Weather

Also by Holly Prado

Nothing Breaks Off at the Edge (New Rivers Press)
Feasts (Momentum Press)
Losses (Laurel Press)
How the Creative Looks Today (The Jesse Press)
Gardens, a novel (Harcourt Brace)
Specific Mysteries (Cahuenga Press)
Esperanza: Poems for Orpheus (Cahuenga Press)
These Mirrors Prove It (Cahuenga Press)
Monkey Journal (Tebot Bach Press)
From One to the Next (Cahuenga Press)
Oh, Salt/ Oh, Desiring Hand (Cahuenga Press)
Really Truly, Autobiographies (Green Tara Press)

Holly Prado

Weather

a poem/ a chronicle

cahuenga

PRESS

Acknowledgments

First Edition ISBN13: 978-0-9851843-4-6 ISBN10: 0-9851843-4-5
Library of Congress Control Number: 2019903117
Prado, Holly, 1938–2019.

Front and back cover photos *Clouds over Woodland Hills*,
and back cover photo of author by: Harry E. Northup

Book Design and Typesetting: Ellison/Goodreau
Printed by: McNaughton and Gunn, Inc., Saline, MI, USA

Cahuenga Press is owned, financed and operated by its poet-members James Cushing, Phoebe MacAdams Ozuna, Harry E. Northup and Holly Prado Northup. Our common goal is to create fine books of poetry by poets whose work we admire and respect; to make poetry actual in the world in ways which honor both individual creative freedom and cooperative support.

Cahuenga Press
1223 Grace Dr.
Pasadena, CA 91105
www.cahuengapress.com

Table of Contents

YEAR ONE

YEAR TWO

YEAR THREE

This Book Is For Harry E. Northup, My Husband
"Loyalty, heat, admiration and sometimes total
collapse from the surprise brought by love –
Our private harvest of sun in our bodies grown
suddenly stronger, suddenly bold."

Thanks to the many writers who trusted me with
their work during the fifty-one years I taught classes
and workshops. Every one of those writers brought
us all closer to a liveable world through their
devotion to the creative act. Thanks, also, to the
members of the journal writing workshop who have
come together for more than thirty years to share
their lives through writing. Their devotion to
personal truth proves that clear-eyed honesty always
defeats hatred, prejudice, devisiveness and shame.

The particulars: I spend them as they come to me,
which is never loss but accumulation, page after
page. I had a stone from Duino which burned in a
fire: Rilke's angel, who remembers, still, who is ready
to be found as mystery's endless language, eager to
speak of itself.

Weather

NOW, WE GO FORWARD

1.

but where? My old friend writes
me a nasty goodbye. I don't even know where he lives
since he and his partner split up. So, "forward" erases
the street names, and here's what I see:

the top of a palm tree whose dangling fronds rattle and shift.
Autumn pretends to mean rest — loss of bitterness, sweat
and resentment. But today I sit up in bed, look at the palm,
which is brittle from drought, wonder how anything makes up
its future from death. My old friend Tony thinks that he hates me.

I remind him our young season's gone. I remind
my own body.

My saviors were poets and poems, wilderness, ouija, flame
burning a long set of dreams, taking a long time — just like
the palm tree — cracking, uprooting. I couldn't stand
my own family, the sternness they served. Now,

we go forward. I want Tony at home, friend who, in the Sixties,
got me stoned, got me off to a concert, got me to dance and to cook.
Told me (when he sought out astrology) I'd live to be an old lady.
He saw this as we sat on the steps of a house where I wouldn't live
for much longer. Who knows what he saw? He just said I'd be
an old lady. I am an old lady. I'm the top of the palm tree, rubbing
itself on itself.

Tony brought out a ouija board once, so we tried it.
It gave me the truth: a future ruined by a woman,
dark haired. I found such hair in the bathroom I shared with
my unfaithful husband, three years after the ouija had told me.
Soothsaying, skrying, fortunes and trance. Dinners and birthdays:

Tony hates aging. I know he believes that he hates me.
We've been friends because we can't live without risk. I fling
myself onto this page without caring who listens, who's
already fled, bored with my wail and my syntax; he takes
his life to – at last report – Mongolia, somewhere as
strange and as gorgeous as that. His home address?
Will I see him again?

* * * * *

October: the month Wallace Stevens was born, same date
that Marla, first muse, has her birthday. October: When
Stevens wrote poems against sadness, he offered that sadness
along with its solace. When Marla entered my life wearing
black tights and beret, she insisted I buy a small laughing
Buddha made out of wood, "very old," said the man at the counter,
eager to hurry the purchase. I would have said no, the money's
too much, but I was about to enter the world, in need
of a Buddha to steady my feet. Marla was theater,
coffee house folk songs, sex before sex was allowed.
I paid for the Buddha; I drank black espresso.

Now, every morning, I touch my old hands to the hands
of a Buddha Tony once brought from Cambodia. A tall wooden
Buddha – I press my hands to his hands, ask him to take care of Tony.
Buddhas adhere to this house, whether or not I am Buddhist:
My original laughing small statue, along with a cat Buddha,
fully enlightened. Also, the white plaster one out on the patio
left behind because it was broken when somebody moved.
I filled the cracked belly with smooth, rounded stones,
not willing to discard a Buddha. Not able to let go of friendship.

2.

The moon says October, month when we bow to our dead;
read from their poems to whomever will listen.
Books made of ego; books made of spit;
books made of nothing like caution or whisper.

October: wind-twist from Libra to Scorpio, dragon
of water and sky — we look down as the well hears us
drop in our wishes; we look through sky into heaven,
wishing there, too, for stars to let secrets come toward us.
We move forward without our permission. We move where
the water drowns all our pennies, where heaven has brought us eclipse:
eclipse of the Moon Mother, consumed by our shadow. Dragon's
long, multiple tongues. My friend's words: Rejection and cold.

My father, a Libra. Marla, a Libra. Tony, a Libra.
Tough balance, those indifferent scales held far above us.
This morning, my father's clear face as if in a photo
taken before he collapsed, died so quickly no one
could reach him in time. His final rejection of me:
no loving goodbye.

Libra to Scorpio:
We smell the dark soil; we listen to crawling and hissing.
Who took the sugar of language? Summer's huge peaches?
I can't get that taste on my tongue; the month of the dragon
has seared possibility down to what's leveled and burned.

3.

Here's what I don't understand:
Why do I love ancient Egypt more
than I love my own father? Today,

I visited mummies, a special exhibit,
respectfully researched, everything *us* —

I felt no difference between that and alive little
children hooting outside on the museum's broad patio.

We test every muscle we have, grateful for movement,
for being, because it might not last through the winter.
My father, dead in November; my child's adoration dead, too.
I'm not the stalwart, professional woman he spent
long-saved money to send off to college. College?
I was his excellent student. But I was preparing
to call my own dragon down from the sky,
from what I didn't believe I could bear.
Dear Dad, I meant all the anguish I caused you.

4.

Grace: One American thing we can't earn.
One human prayer never answered.

Grace falls to us — lapful of fruit, sudden release from the tree.
Nothing we've done can deserve this. No one we've helped
makes a difference. Clean dishes, clean bedroom corners,
clean conscience: Nothing brings Grace except Grace.

Today, it's all loss striking my cheeks —

the sharp, murky air of LA October, the not-so-great
salad at lunch when I wanted the taste of luxurious
vegetables, not second-rate grocery store stuff.
Grace? Given to those who deserve nothing.

The season turns from peaches to heavy Bosc pears.
Hallowe'en pumpkin, potful of lilies along with a green, toothy bat.
But attention to detail isn't a clue to divine intervention.
Cynicism's a sin, yet gentle acceptance is filled with its own snaky hell.
I ate the dull salad; I spent too much time thinking of it,
of my low expectations for lunch, for forgiveness,

of uses of language as in the recent French film
which was oh-so-despairing while looking so stylish
I almost bought into its crap. Scorpio: ever the dragon,
ever the wrestling with poisonous instincts. October,
soul-maker, frightener, sweet-bringer – the candy
we shove in our mouths to forget what we know.

No, we are better than that. We bow to our dead.
We tell them their poems so they won't be lonely.
We gather to form a clear circle: remember, remember.
Once, after the death of a poet who'd been part of my circle
of poets, I heard many crows out on the telephone line
who cawed and who cawed until I went out, listened to them,
the urgency surely the poet herself: twenty huge crows,
twenty long poems. Their voices were gospel: Remember.

5.

The mummies: Ancient Egypt, Ancient Peru, artful respect shown
to loved ones – we've always had loved ones. In Peru,
whole family groups settle in burial bundles, in caves,
always together, resting right next to each other. I don't know
where my mother's ashes are buried. I was too young to ask.
My father is scattered all through the ocean. I will be, too,
though my astrological sign is the earth.
But I don't want to be in the ground.

I want release. The unchangeable past – that tight-woven
shawl – dropped, trampled, decayed.

6.

We've come to Hallowe'en. This year
is cooking and art: corn pudding, pork roast;

Olivia's print – burnt orange, wine-red – eruptive,

while her gold sky becomes home: Olivia's art. Olivia's friendship
secure in her studio up on a hill where I know I can find her.

Dinner, then kids wanting candy,
wax fangs which I buy every year.
Let's have some fun. Then,

the whole day, sunlight and all, comes undone.
Here are the gods of the dead; here are the ancestor
spirits; here is my grandmother's handpainted platter
ready to serve up November's Thanksgiving turkey.
Our dead are in Heaven. Or in the vast Underworld:
Hades, great God of Souls has welcomed our absent
ones kindly. And we who are living have fields
we call Elysian — Elysian Park where Olivia walks here in LA.:
above city hall, above Dodger Stadium, above freeways and noise
there is something Elysian and blessed: Olivia's studio,
painter's retreat, a place to create what's never
been in our world before this. What's art?
Intention and practice. What's death? I've never
been dead. Prophecy? Ouija? Astrology's logic, based on
the movement of planets? I believe all of that
more than I think investing in stocks is a solid idea.

* * * * *

Tony said I'd be an old lady. I take off my clothes
before I can sleep; I see my old body — the rain-starved old fronds
that the palm shakes and clatters: it's my frantic old soul who looks up,
expecting the best, rewarded with nothing but more of November.

7.

November Moon: her darkest self, never defined, brings me a dream:
my mother, who says I've ignored her, haven't been helpful.

Mother, you're dead.

You've never been able to help me.
Why do you need me to sweep, to pick up the crumbs?

When I was sixteen, you were the sickest you'd ever be.
I couldn't help then; I was a fury of hormones,
had crushes on boys who wore black leather jackets.
How was I going to clean up your desperate cancer,
your own mother's silence, your thin ugly hair which barely
covered your head? How could I, embarrased by everything
womanly I would come into, give comfort?

Comfort? Tonight, November 13th, 2015, we're getting
the news out of Paris about terrorist attacks. Suicide
bombers taking the lives of themselves and Parisians.
The constant TV repeats and repeats its long comments
which bring us no clear understanding of hatred,
of murder: religion that's never religious.

Tony, where are you living in this broken world?
I know you love Paris.

One witness said, "Pools of blood.
Not drops. Pools of blood." Then, he cried.

* * * * *

I don't like Thanksgiving. I don't like the snotty
stand-up comedian doing her schtick on TV,
her political rant, stupid and pointless. Or the worry
I have about being alive in November, when nothing
goes well. "Radicalized" is the word I hear over and over.
Meaning suicide bombers. Meaning beheadings. Meaning slavery and rape.

I have nothing but pain to give to my mother.
Nothing but loss to present to this month
when the sky is as dark as the moon, early so early.

Now we go forward, but where?

We'll soon have December. Our sky, which was promising
rain, is blue-gray, but the sun powers into this room
with its back-of-my-neck-warming fingers. I'm grateful for that.

* * * * *

We hoard what we can against winter, no matter how warm
it is here in LA. We shore up the harvest, the holiday presents,
This day has been decent to me; I haven't stumbled, broken
already disorderly bones. I've been with good women who write,
whose elegant faces show wear. Out in the huge autumn sky,
leonid meteors give us their message: Don't think too much
of your human pursuits. Don't think you won't be
dissolved in everything wilder than you. Enter
your myths with your open-palmed hands on your knees.

I see in my mind one of the women whose losses have
taken her body under itself, hunching her over until
when she writes her chest is touching the page.
We rub ourselves into the paper, the trees it all came from.

I mount a resistance to shopping, to ads, to false jingle bells
bringing false-bearded Santas who chuckle false ho ho until I want
simply the end of November, end of the dragon,
beginning of slamming my mind against luxury items, against fabulous trash.
I don't have to buy into Santa or Rudolph or eggnog on sale
or buy a new car to smash up when everyone's drunk.

That witness in Paris after the ISIS attacks: his face plain,
undefended: "Pools of blood. Pools of blood."

8.

The Pilgrims risked life to gain purity.
Why was it purity that would redeem them?
Why not art?
Why not poetry: a small memorial notice

in this morning's obituaries: one of our poets,
one of our own, always loved for her merciless shout –
Okay, yes, pure as the twenty pure crows
who gathered after she died. This morning,

Thanksgiving morning, one crow balances, black
and resilient, out on the telephone wire. He caws
because things are okay. The world is on fire, but here
on this street in East Hollywood, we're okay. Harry, my husband,
comes in from his walk, says he's seen Robert and Sergio,
two shattered neighbors. He's glad they're still with us,
alive and, for now, reasonably sane. You never know.

You never imagine where synapses squander your brain,
make you leap over the boundary into the maelstrom.
We're often so close to that edge; we're often so close
to our anguish and shouting and flying off wires without the black crow's
steady, grand wings. Human existence: thankfulness sliced like
the big roasted turkey – one day to eat; the next one to stare at your fingers,
counting them over and over to be sure they're all there. Maybe they're not.

What did the Pilgrims
do with their minds to stay sane?

                    * * * * *

The Pilgrims drank beer. They said prayers.
They killed one bad Indian, hung his head
on a post for the neighbors to see. Miles Standish
was with them; he'd fought in the Thirty Years War.
He was brutal. What else can you be when your loved ones
sicken and die, when you're driven to propping them up in the forest,

frozen, guns shoved into their arms? Dead guards.
Dead babies. Dead women: John Bradford's wife
fell off the Mayflower while it was at anchor;
a three-year-old child had just died. Maybe she jumped.

Tony, tell me you love what you're doing, wherever
you are. Tell me you're warm, have new shirts, eat bowls
filled with rices and herbs. Your laugh comes from your throat;
you never contain it; you put your head on your arm while your laughter
goes through you. You can laugh at disasters – you've helped me
through several. You can expound. You can talk about music.
Music and music and music. The first time we did something social
together we went to a classical concert – piano – a famous musician,
superb. Tony, tell me you're not gobbling pills anymore.
Not drinking so much. The Pilgrims managed to claw through those
first awful years on Cape Cod, finally grow corn.

Tony, tell me something delicious is growing for you.
Tell me you're laughing.

9.

It's December: I stand on the edge between
fatal nostalgia and goodbye forever. Here in my half-empty garden,
I dig locked-in roots – once vibrant rose-mint geranium, sprawling now,
lacking in scent – I dig through dark soil while this month posts closing time
right on the door. Everything shuffles away; everything hushes in shock:

There's been more violence, more sale of firearms.
"To take care of my family," one man says,
shouldering his just-bought, long-barreled gun.
How is he ending the year? How will he celebrate?
By shooting a stranger who walks on *his* street,
passing *his* house, *his* family, his notion of *his*?

What *is* his? What is ours? When I shove my hands
into these potsful of soil, what am I trying to find?
I want to cradle the stuff that my fish-pawed first
ancestor stepped on the moment he thought to be human.
I want to be human, planting next spring more rose-mint
geraniums, something I need to see live.

* * * * *

More wind than I can keep out of the house. Small
leaves – veined, tannish, touched with fierce red –
travel into the living room, into the kitchen.
I recognize death, final or just rich in metaphor.
So be it. So, I think, as I put my ear to the incoming wind,
be it. Leaves plummet toward us: The old Chinese elm,
which doesn't belong to this property, but thinks of itself as
something we need. Its branches clutter the roof of our house.
Its leaves are all over our floors now, because we're in
December when everything shifts from foundation
to flight. This afternoon, I sat with my plants and

looked up. Looked so far into sky that there was no sky,
only cloud, white white cloud, white sliding and wisping
and fast disappearing. White: Absence of color. Absence
of body. Absence of thought. I couldn't move
until I, too, was absent. Just gone.

* * * * *

Season of dreams; here's mine from last night:

A photographer wants me to pose nude with many
fresh vegetables. I protest that my stomach's too large
to be artful. "That's what I love," the photographer
says. "Your big stomach."

Mythic nude woman, huge-bellied, our Venus of Willendorf.
I'm not that myth, but I'm moved by what women inherit: our bellies.

The Venus of Willendorf, twenty-five thousand years old, still moves
our blank hearts when we think how many children come from
reminding ourselves of the feminine body we need to exist.
I dream my own place among vegetables, fruits,
ancestor limestone and ochre. Nothing in dreaming is wasted.
Nothing in history is crime but refusal to grasp your own place,

your own sacred words, your special hot soil.

10.

Winter solstice. Rain. Willingness to drive far across the city
for lunch with friends, lunch in a restaurant heady with holiday
specials and views of each other's full plates. There's not
too much traffic; not too much anguish,
except for the homeless, who are not in the restaurant,
not eating sand dabs and salmon and handmade ice cream.

I look out to the patio when we get home: new table,
new succulents. My smallest of small tributes to Nature,
to winter here in LA. Things grow all year around;
the rosemary thrives. The parsley laps up the rain.
My husband sustains poetry, love and long friendship.
This is the most anyone holds: faith in the home we already have.

* * * *

Early this Christmas morning, wheeling and shining
out in the fine light blue sky: sea gulls, numerous
sea gulls, far from the ocean but close to our
neighborhood Christmas. Their turning draws ever more
shine to the underside wings of the birds.

One man on the street while I'm watching the gulls:
He's wrapped in his bathrobe, wears sandals with socks.
He's the one person walking the street, going wherever he's going,
wearing his bathrobe, his non-self, self before there is any
strict distance between him and the big public world,
which demands jackets, haircuts, closed shoes.

Christmas we make of ourselves, of the first things we see,
along with re-reading my journal – the year's end
recorded as breakage, as loyalty. Puzzlement,
anger, stupid mistakes and forgiveness.

Christmas evening, full moon lingers, befriending cold sky.
Astrology translates itself into Capricorn –
death of the old king, birth of the new: incarnation as
mother, as matter, as earth. Here we are, alive in the quick
time we have, the view of our Christmas full moon, pale
white, now tenderly fading, leaving it all in our too-human
hands. The task: Live on the edge *between fatal nostalgia
and goodbye forever.* I fill in my own wisdom's calendar
for the new year; I trust days will fall in numerical order,
but who can rely even on that?

SHINE

1.

No more that year: We've wrung what it had
from its body, buried it under bitter and comfort.

This new year's morning, I sit up in bed —
shocked in the tough winter sunlight which
gives me this news: Our angels are taking
a break; it's now up to us. Harry has a new camera;

I look for his photos to be revelation.
They are, I believe:
big photos of shirts on a fence, colors and stripes
meant for sale. Church parking lot's sign forbids us to park.
Homelessness, homelessness. East Hollywood torn
from its night, set out before us:

Why not, then, at least try to find love,

love enormous as sunshine, dangerous when you look
at its face but kind when its soft, startling paw turns
my poor shoulder toward just what I know how to do?

* * * * *

Rain finally arrives, speaks like a relative home from the wars —
full of harsh stories and crying. We need such infusion, although
it can flood us, carry away houses, our cars. We open the oven,
feed rain what's been waiting: stews and large meats.

We have to be bold, exhibit our faith even as torrents chew on
our hems. One poet has Lupus; several are intimate sufferers; three
now can't walk without falling. We cluster. We talk. "Language," I say,
over and over, "language is ours."

One year ago, murders at Charlie Hebdo, radical hatred killing
the thing that just won't be killed: word-saying, word-writing;
word upon word in the face of what hates human speech,
open thought. My husband's camera brings home our local news:

shopping carts, loaded with goods, parked next to tall metal cabinets
graffitied, including one pure white dove. Then, the acre of lovely, calm cult:
Self Realization, its white/gold/super-clean buildings remind me
that everyone comes to this city for rescue — the gift shop's sweet incense,
or a torn plastic bag in the cart, holding somebody's blanket. "Can you stay warm?"
I ask Elliott, homeless and helpful to me: watering plants, carrying whatever is heavy
for us. "I found a cubbyhole," Elliott says. His front teeth are gone. He praises God;
he feels redeemed. But he doesn't visit his ex and their children because
she might fight with him, might call the cops.

First thing this morning, here's a recycling truck, a T Rex, armored
and rumbling and urgent in picking up bins full of plastic we didn't need
to begin with; rumbling and crunching, eating us up, re-making the junk
into I-don't-know-what, but doing its job. Forcing some change in the
world shape, the present, the time in our heads, the Gulf Stream, the
drifting apart of the planets, African misery, Syrian misery, American
wish to revise and restore.

What a failure we are when transfiguration is all about plastic.

Sergio, neighbor, self-defined "guardian" here on our street;
Sergio, oddly atuned, keeper of discarded goods; Sergio, who's spent
his whole life in that house I have never been in, right across
from our own:

Sergio has cancer, has hospice, is waiting to die, to be taken into
another procession — matter made cloud, made florescence.

What a difference for him. But I believe Sergio will be around,
like the ghost who inhabits our group of apartments. This man
has appeared to the neighbors; I've seen swift, fleeting darkness
the shape of a shirt sleeve. Death? Serious stuff. Or, maybe not.

Some ghosts are enormous, some are tiny but brave. The theme here
is crushing harsh angers I couldn't get rid of in autumn, kneeling to love,
whatever its shape: Cures may include dying, then dying, then dying again.

2.

Cures may include Beethoven's grand string quartets.

Or Harry, who says as I write, "You're just where you
want to be." Or the small Buddha fountain out on the patio,
next to one gray-green, plump-leafed new succulent:
It sets out a fresh little bit of itself, some pure need to be upright.
Nature, indifferent and brash, can take, too, a gentler path.

2 AM: I come out of sleep because I hear voices: men
talking outside, consonant blur except for these words:
"right now," which I hear all the way from my need for
Beethoven's music through sleep to the surge
of the morning's requirements and hopes.

* * * * *

Why aren't we sobbing in gratitude, thanking the planets —
five in alignment right now, five powers listening — for sanity,
household, subscription renewals, buying Bosc pears whenever
we want their curving expanse firm on our counters? Street
protests rage. Unfair. Unfair. Nothing is fair. I know it. I hate injustice
myself, but here are Mercury, Venus, Saturn and Mars. Jupiter, too,
lined up in the sky: Magic, Love, Stern Rigor and Power —

such conjured forces keeping us settled, in place, able to speak
in clear sentences. This year's first month can see toward its end

holding love as the thread through the maze. One of my small
watercolors covered with hearts, just like fourth grade, painted
in red, pasted in gold. This was for Harry. He wanted to know
how to flatten the paper. I said, "Let it dry for awhile,"
a solution so plain, so nothing-to-do, I felt childhood again,
where problems were *here* – and then gone. Harry's been

out with his camera: Virgen de Guadalupe, her candles –
24 to a box, boxes stacked up in our 99¢ Store. Her mantle:
holy blue-green. The halo behind her concocted of sunlight, of fire.
Comfort's combustion, Divine Adoration: odd-smelling roses not of this life –
roses left by the Virgen when she appeared to a peasant who needed a task:
"Build me a church." He'd been a pagan, a medicine man, and I'm sure
he still was. No holy mother seeks out an idiot.

I find a poem I'd forgotten I'd written – about the invisible world,
its attendance on us. "Fear Not!" calls the memory of some old bad movie
and perfect for just how I breathe, unafraid in these final four days
of the month that can't speak for themselves but rest in those planets
staying aligned until what comes next:

* * * * *

Our angels return from vacation.

* * * * *

What's worth imagining? What's worth achieving? What do you
think of the weather this week – rain promised but not yet arrived?
What squeaks as it opens the old closet door? What heals a raw day?
The salad bowl breaks but not the large Corning Ware dish I've
had since the late 1960s, gift from a previous mother-in-law
who made flour torillas first thing in the morning. She had no
questions about what she was doing or how she should live.
How could I understand anyone certain, combined with strong
faith in her family, her church, her good taste in the kitchen
equipment she gave me as gifts? The salad bowl breaks,

but not the reminder that some people have all the answers.
I can't say I'm glad to be left in the blind fucking dark,
but as much as the Corning Ware dish means to me,
I'm okay not knowing what to expect.

Sunday, the weather predicts, will bring rain.
Monday will tear us apart with its Renaissance clouds,
and, yes, I see angels: They're sighing, wishing they
didn't have to go back to work, but we rely on their laughter.

3.

Sergio's dead. He died on the 12th of last month,
month of god Janus who looks forward and back;
twelve a high number of wholeness, completion.

Another young man is dead of the drugs
he loved more than his children, more than himself.

Judy, Harry's old high school companion — she's
gone. A young friend of a friend: dying right now.
The husband of someone I cherish: a brain tumor's
ending his life. I want

love as the living, strong blood thrumping our hearts
to rule this new year, but Death makes a place for Itself,
always a place at the newly-set table, wiping Its mouth
on one of those lovely, soft linen napkins. Death is the
first angel back from the spa, willing to share our good
food, our cheap wine. Whatever we're having, Death's
having it, too. The toppling wine glasses fall to the floor.
Shards and fine slivers, crystal geometry scatter
across the sudden new year; I hardly can bear sweeping them
into the trash — because art's always made from the broken;
or, it's made like Beethoven's 3rd String Quartet, his best years
encouraging spiffy new clothes, dance lessons and love.
He'd only begun to go deaf. He'd only begun to be mentioned

with Mozart and Haydn. Let's let him have these good times,
an embroidered new vest, a kiss saying more than goodnight.

Today, I've asked for Sergio's comfortable passage to whatever is next.
I've organized moon watercolors by date; I've made swordfish
tacos. I wear a large yellow sweatshirt that serves its best purpose:
keeping me warm, in spite of its age and shapeless condition.
Today starts the Year of the Monkey,

lunar assault, new moon as a swift, darting eye that Monkey
assures us sees everything we might not find. Monkey:
Bring us your news, let us be curious, just as you are.
The quick-acting Monkey isn't so differerent from our Holy Virgen,

her appearance exactly in front of the man she had chosen to build her a church.
What will be built in this simian year? What kind of promise does Monkey
think we'll enjoy? Orange tangerines come into their best season yet:

The most enlightened enjoyment so far has been this: I cradle
the fruit with both hands, amazed at how easy it is to discover the
edible segments, how quickly the rind drops, how much our food
needs us, giving out sweetness and vitamins — all that it's got —
to keep us alive.

4.

Nothing is partial. Each side has the other. Now, we are halfway
through love's fertile month, when spirits wake up to the
red in our closets: blouses forgotten and shoes we've ignored.
Valentine's Day: I work on a book; why am I sure about my own past?
I'm sure because each act I describe is shaped by what never could happen —
those opposites mingled, fermenting. If I can't help but lie, it's the truth:

It's always the red circle skirt I had on when I twirled to the music
from "Carmen," played on the radio when I was ten. I was becoming
a full Spanish opera, written in French. Deceit in that story, but fabulous
beauty, applause for performance, for mythic fatality. Nothing adults said

made sense, but I understood sopranos and costumes.

What can you offer that's truer than "Carmen"?

* * * * *

I take Harry's picture; he's standing in front of the writing
I manage this morning, after quick, nasty illness for both
of our stomachs. We are much better; he's going out
for a walk, blue scarf at his throat. The weather is after-rain
emerald weeds in the neighborhood yards, with, right now,
a red pickup truck zipping by on our street. "Right now,"
those words coming out of last month, 2 AM hushed conversation
outside our house, but "right now" as clear as an angel's return:

The Beethoven Angel, who has decided she wants him
included, no matter my preference for Bartok.
But I honor the privilege of this last string quartet
I'm hearing right now and right now and right now as
the strings create full, somber mercy. I've been looking
for solace. The new Zika virus deforms unborn babies;
a new peace treaty flops; even Pope Francis blasts politicians
who aren't all-inclusive. Beethoven sends violins to that
prayer-zone where nothing's denied: then, a small dance. Then,
a whole wedding — blend and rejoice. Then, who knows what
he's thinking; everything crashes and shrieks. But not without
one final, beautiful chord to assure me that rain — self centered,
abrupt — cares enough to return.

* * * * *

The medical waiting room, strangers together,
all sufferers, stoic and quiet. A four-year-old boy
straddles two chair-arms, rides them, makes
soft, chugging sounds. He is so pleased with
himself, so glad to be here with his mother,
with round glasses to see through. When a nurse
calls his family, he waves to her — gently,

a small wave of pleasure because he is sure
that whoever comes into his life means
well, is worthy of welcome.

I make nothing of this except to remind
my own sorrow that there has been, today,
a child who topples my doubt, who even
has dimples and, now, evening, is pajamaed
and sleeping. He is love's bravery, trust in the nurse
who will usher his hard-limping mother into
a room where a doctor will help her.

I sit now and listen to Harry, who's home from a walk.
"Thank you, camera," he says. His photo at night:
Self-Realization Fellowship domes, golden, shining
in spite of nothing to gain, no one who's coming to worship.
Just gold, just black sky. My black ink, tracing these lines
through what helps and what squats on its terrible
haunches, daring my efforts.

Our patio Buddha —

white, laughing, stones in his cracked-
open belly. When Harry photographs
him and the gnome and stone rabbit,
the succulents growing around them,
that's plenty of truth for today, Leap
Year Day — noon now, end of the
month, March flowing in on Moon's
waning and Monkey's swift glance.

5.

I pick parsley. Moon moves through
Capricorn, a time to set goals.

I never have goals; I only have fate and a book list,

parsley and candles. Here's something I know:
I can say "tababuia": flowering trees whose blooms
fill our streets every spring. Refusal of modesty –
big, pink, full bosomed trees who might

sneak up behind you to whisper "Resistance is futile!"
We do approach spring, now that it's March.
An equinox fingers its way toward our plans.

My book list? One fabled critic who writes
about Stevens. Also, a handbook: watercolor techniques –

I've learned to paint air.

* * * * *

Third rain: inspires warbling, birds before 6 AM –
solo, then choral achievement. They've been dis-spirited,
dried out, sullen in winter. This morning, as rain gives
us big band insistence, the birds think of mating, of eggs,
of the nests they will hide from the crows.
The birds even now, 8:30 AM, are still at it, still twanging and
and trinkling and wootzing, then smoothing the notes into lovely paté.
They are fabulous, life-giving pilgrims, willing to share their religion of instinct
with anyone needing a way to go on into evening, when, still,
occasional bird tweedle and flute extend from a tree above dinner.

* * * * *

The angels, still wary, return, but they're taking their time.
They don't like uneven skies, too familiar these days.
The Angel of Death and the Beethoven Angel are brave and
immortal. Less prominent guardians wait for assignments;
some never are called to do good. All, though, believe in their duties
but stumble and weep, like the children they were. They keep locks
of their dead mothers' hair tucked in their robes to remind them that they, too,
have been human.

Elliott comes to water the plants on the patio. "Lightly,"
I tell him. "We may have more rain."

"You can take half of this back." He holds out the twenty
I've handed to him. "Keep it. As long as I can afford it,

why not?" Maybe someday I won't have enough extra
to pay him. We agree: we're just lucky to wake up
every morning, to still be alive. "God gives us such beauty
to look at. When we're dead, we won't see it," he says.

"Maybe we'll see beauty that's different. We don't know.
Death is *the* mystery, isn't it?" Elliott nods. "Yeah, it sure is."

So, I start this March 10th with theology, generosity,
eggs from chickens raised by Kathleen and Larry.
If I despair; if I'm exhausted; if I can't bear this vicious political year;
I can count on domestic/philosophical rescue, however it
comes to the door. Life's greatest mantra: Be patient and wait.

6.

March 15th, the Ides of March, the ominous center.
End of beginning: to Romans, final new year's festivities,
and, of course, Julius Caesar's assassination.

But today, this March 15th, 2016,

we have sun, along with repairs. Phone, now restored,
working again as it should. Two friends not feeling well,
but this isn't death in the streets. This is our simple, secure
daily lives. We can dial 911. We can slip on sunglasses
to keep out the glare. By mid-afternoon, I'm eating
some salad, then taking a nap. It's "Super Tuesday,"
political uproar. We're electing a President, not
murdering one. But, yes, there's still murder, fierce war,
refugees streaming from Syria onto Greek shores,

then heading wherever they can. Mud and no tents and

TV footage of children, their facial expressions no longer
unknowing but worried: Their foreheads in creases, babies
stare at the camera. Spring has only a few days to wait.
What can it bring to these babies, symbols of spring and rebirth?

* * * * *

My recent dreams re-organize pieces of fabric,
of cardboard, anything in me needing new shape.
What I know now is *try*, shift every scrap I am given,
respond to the tasks hoping, they will, yes, make sense.

Spring arrives in this present March on the chilly 19th.
It takes a few days for the workmen next door to put down
their drills and their buzz saws, start singing a popular song.
It takes spring herself quite awhile to release her pale feet
from the dank residue of her underworld winter.

In the meantime,
too many emails and phone calls fracture my time.
I'm happy to come to this writing, see a blank page
below the lines I've already lived. The blank mind
is a wonderful tool. Here's what I dream
to answer the multiple scraps:

Harry and I stare up at a moon in a darker than
dark, pure black sky. Even the moon is all black,
except for a curve at the bottom that's glistening silver,
everything sparkling we need.

This is the meaning of "shine."

"Shine" from Old English "scinan," to be radiant,
to shed light. Then, swiftly,

it's Easter, from Eastre, Teutonic goddess of dawn.

YEAR ONE, PART THREE: April, 2016 — June, 2016

THIS SIMIAN YEAR

1.

What can I do that I'm not doing now?
The old monkey-mothers tell what they know, but I hear so little.

* * * *

Once, a strange child looked from a staircase
into my eyes. She was a creature, not one of us.
Where did she come from? She'd be a young
woman by now, sniffing out sex and work
she can do with her hands. She's not a thinker;
she follows her eyes, which travel without
her permission. They watch a man's crotch
as he makes his way toward her. When she smiles,
her teeth come forward a little. Often,

creation forgets to be tender. Our births
don't have to love us. Our parents don't
have to be female and male but an Otherness
hidden behind that fat bush over there.
Someone I know had sex with her brother
her whole teenage life. We turn away,
but she opened her legs. Boundaries have wavering edges:

Once, I dreamed African jungle, a place
where I walked through a gate, onto a
path leading into unseeable distance.
I wanted to walk; I wanted to know all
the lushness, the silence. Then, I felt

many eyes watching me. They saw that I didn't belong.
The jungle was ancient, and tree-made. I was too human.

* * * * *

Marla is dying. First muse, college roommate,
burden and friend – reminder, annoyance, her
beauty a ruin, yet precious, as ruins often are.
Early on, she pushed toward theatrical life. She
almost became that woman, the actor she longed to be.

Cliché a bright star, burning out. It's all I can
think of to say what "almost" includes.
Right now, a bad kidney; a bang on her head
dislodging her reason. Bad teeth. Bad decisions.

Marla: bold ring on her finger, the one that she gave me:
silver, with masks on each side: tragedy/comedy.
After I wore it awhile, the ring broke in half.
I kept the two parts, as if they might come together
by magic. The last time I looked, both halves were gone.

I simply knew how to work. I thought my innate, stubborn
dullness was all that I had, but diligence has its own charms:
I understand alphabets, typing, page turning –
how to number those pages once they are written.

* * * * *

Again, Marla's not ready to die; that will occur in another two years.
She's nearly died more than once. What does her life need from her now?
More years won't bring her health or reunion with sons who don't
want to see her. But the Fates take their time. Sometimes, they're
indifferent; sometimes, sweet-tempered. None of us knows which it will be.

2.

Birds, birds, lots of many many birds in the rainy,
blank weather. The birds are a million years older than me.
What made the choice to give us a language but nothing like wings?
The rain isn't thinking of us; it only loves birds.

Mid-April. Harry sees pigeons mating
outside our window. Each year, male puffing up,
female reluctance. One mockingbird must
have a nest in the vines at the end of the driveway;

It visits, re-visits the vines. There must be eggs there – hidden, secure.

Eventually, both of the pigeons fly up,
fly away with each other. Such urgent promise.

Spring: the least reasonable moment we have –
the mail bringing praise, but a car gets a ticket
for parking where city officials decide it should
leave. Somebody pays me too much but says
it's okay, but yesterday right up on Edgemont a man
shot a woman he wanted to love. Then, he
evaded police the whole morning: sirens
and searches. It's spring. Don't buy a gun.
Fall directly in love with someone
you don't need to maim.

"Baseball and poetry." Harry speaks up Sunday morning
before I've had coffee or breakfast. He repeats: "Baseball
and poetry." Then, later, he reads aloud: Whitman inhabits
our house, along with the Dodgers and Harry's own writing.
I gave my father all Whitman's poems,

my gift on one Christmas. He gave them back. I still have that book –
"To Dad," inscribed on the flyleaf. I was in high school.
My mother had died. My father had already lost me to writers,
to art, to a future of myth and of story – of two masks hanging

now in our study: One a carved goat god of wood; one of the moon,
silver, her mouth as if waiting, as if she will lean down to taste us.

* * * * *

I watch what changes. Clouds at this moment: clutching each other,
slow foreplay and tango. Now, separation – the partners dissolve;
the future: white mist. Earlier, full moon through the bedroom.
It woke me up. What do we all want to do? Stretch toward what's lost?
Think it can bring itself back to our arms?

My birth gave me Midwestern prairie, that stolid
pioneer braiding my hair, making its lunches of bison,
of wheat. What did I need from my childhood? To leave it.
The passage was permanent – breasts, hips and underarm odor.
Girls couldn't be cowboys. My wish for a horse dropped to the dirt
along with my plan to star in the movies. There was blood on my panties
each month. I was told I'd have babies. Don't let boys touch me.
But they wanted to touch me. What should I do? Pay attention to
boys or to my sane mother whose protection I cherished? Oh,
boys, though. Who guided my staring outside my bedroom,
the window revealing nothing but satisfied houses,
small lawns, the street gliding up to a busier street. Once,
I dreamed that the sidewalk next to the street lay covered with snakes.
I had to ease my way through them, not step on their coiling.

Me, a twelve-year-old girl, stepping between reptilian
knowledge toward the busier street, the place where my puppy
was killed, run over and killed before he could even grow into
my dog, a companion between the strange snakes and my strange adult
self. I was alone in my dream, in my bedroom, alone in my well-
meaning, irrelevant family, alone as I looked from my window,
as if the right message would come on the side of a truck,
or on a cloud, or shouted from an old man on the block,
one of whom gave me a Savings Bond during The Second World War.
Which America won. Which I was supposed to be proud of forever.
But when there were boys, snakes and no cowboy life,
I had enough war in myself to wonder who'd ever win.

3.

What can I do that I'm not doing now?

These wind-crushed days of late April:
Here's evening sun so violently bright through
the window I can't make out houses or driveways,
but only a struggling woman hunched over
a small folding cart, pulling her groceries against too-brilliant
sun, the punishing wind. Her light-weight pink coat,
flapping, lifts out behind her. As the woman's thin coat
spreads away from her body; she won't stop
to wrap it around her but simply keeps going.

I once, myself, stood in the wind:
wind forcing snow in my boots, under
my coat while I waited and waited to get

on a bus. I needed that bus. So, I know
the pink-coated woman; I know her cart
and her groceries. I know what patience
demands — when our young neighbor Allie
borrows a pot to cook pasta, I wonder how
many thousands of meals she'll create before
she's my age. I hope she likes cooking.

* * * * *

Here is a gift for my birthday:

Kwan Yin, compassionate goddess, heavy gray
stone. Graceful, long fingers which languidly fall close to her knee.

Now, a trim Chinese grandmother walks where
the pink-coated woman appeared. This grandmother,
each weekday morning, follows her grandchild to school
at the end of our block. Then, she walks back,
neither hurried nor lagging. She never

insists that the child hold her hand.

This is compassion: To know the right pace.
To not interfere but to be every morning's companion.
The old monkey-mothers watch, too.

* * * * *

Crossing toward, crossing through, crossing a stream
once in the mountains – cold, cold stream filled
with rocks and with water that *rushed,* as we say:

Every time in my life when I've halted to think
what might happen, I've been pushed by that force:

One spring in high school, I volunteered without
thinking I'd volunteered: suddenly ran toward a stage
where a director had asked for a girl to play Cleopatra.
He rolled me into the famous play's rug, and when he
unrolled it, I jumped to my feet, bold Queen of Egypt.

We shouldn't predict even ourselves.

I thought I would go to New York, but I've been
in LA for fifty-six years. I thought I would hover
right next to my life because I lacked courage.
The pushiest Deity finally hurt me so much I
broke off from my small, useless soul; I woke up
to the gift I'd been given: the hills I could see,
my body's revisions –

Unroll the rug – imagine the fun of becoming
unstoppable feminine pleasure and power. I've learned
to have faith in the Push – in the mountains, where
stepping on unsteady rocks got me across that cold water,
got me up to the place

where I camped overnight, then ate oatmeal

for breakfast, oatmeal soaking up rain — my head
with no hat; my face calling "sister" to rain pouring
over my hair and my cheeks.

* * * * *

"Why?" has never been answered for me, so I
wake up wanting only to eat, to see the old
Chinese grandmother: this morning
she has a new jacket; this morning
she's on her way home, having made sure
the child's in a classroom where alphabets'
letters are spelled one at a time, then combined
into thickets, sea waves or tree limbs.
Any real sentence is natural mating.

4.

So, now, Memorial Day, May 30th,
remembering our war dead,
our millions of dead
quiet in their cemeteries,
small flags on the graves.

A child, I heard "Taps" played across the road from
our house in the cemetery full of soldiers killed in World War II.
There would be speeches. My mother made picnics each year.
We'd sit on cemetery grass, listen to how brave the dead had to be.
We'd listen to the dead be quiet. Be absolutely dead.

A national resolution from the year 2000
asks us to pause at 3 PM, Memorial Day,
think for a moment about all the dead. In the past week,

overloaded boats packed with refugees
left Libya for Italy. Some capsized.
A five-year-old boy was found alone;

his mother, brother, sister drowned. He is
surely thinking of the dead. The dead caused
by death's need for more dead, more desperate
boats crammed with poverty, repression,

with bullets and bombing;
with starvation, disease, polluted water.

Shootings in Chicago on May 30th:

more than sixty people dead. A city where
no war is declared, but people shoot
other people? Isn't that what we call war?

5.

June speaks with Juno's voice:
Queen of Heaven – Hera or Frigg
or Mary – this spirit rules the high
point of our year, summer solstice.

Consider summer our neighbor's large cat –
coppery, asleep in some leaves matching its color,
hidden until its closed eyes opened, startling me:

Let us be dazzled by this new Queen of Heaven,
whatever appearance she makes.

* * * * *

Meanwhile, Kim, our friend and cleaning guru,
gardener, bringer today of a plant – tomato, she tells me,
"green and purple heirloom" – Kim has helped me love
this small patio, what can be done with practically nothing.
The little Buddha fountain Kim gave us
rests on the table with a larger Buddha, along with
the other "toys," as Elliott calls them.

I call them guardians.

* * * * *

"Baseball and poetry," Harry says, so last night
we went to Dodger Stadium where Julio Urias
pitched his first Major League home game.
Taking up three rows in front of us:

a whole team, Little League, excited boys who
can't sit still; boys eating snacks – "Share your natchos;
share your natchos with Rodrigo!" one mother
shouts. Boys: more boys, each Dodger shirt
embroided with that kid's name. Everybody wants
to play. Everybody wants to be a Major Leaguer.
Whose arm will be the strongest ten short years from now?
One of them? None of them?

Summer hope.

Summer disaster: In Yellowstone,

someone falls in Norris Geyser Basin,
the oldest, hottest thermal spot: 459 degrees
of fast descent. In seconds, nothing's left of him.

An earthquake – 5.2 – hits Southern California,
hits Borrego Springs right on the San Jacinto fault.
Danger, danger, death and no escape when your
all too human foot, slightly off the given trail,
slips a little, slips a little more.

Or, the earth gives way.

Today, June 12th, West Hollywood's
annual parade: Gay Pride, with floats,
gender flexibility, marvelous costumes,
laughter at our plain gray T-shirts and our

fictions about who can be exactly whom.

In Orlando, Florida, hours before today's
parade, a man opened fire in a gay
nightclub, killed forty-nine. Right now,
helicopters rumble over our East Hollywood.
Protection, surveillance. Because of what?
Pride. Celebrating pride.

* * * * *

End of the solstice month,
Our good Monkey Mothers give one final piece of advice:
Tear up last week's revisions. Nothing is final.

RETURN

1.

Fourth of July: On TV, Smokey Robinson
sings "My Girl'" while hundreds of people
wave their small flags. Smokey looks great,
pokes the mic toward the audience so they'll sing along.

Summertime memory, early and present:
My mother dances the Charleston,
housedress hiked to her thighs. Me,
years later, petting a whale who swims
back to my hand, wanting some more. Harry,
this morning, when I say I'll have peanut
butter — more protein than regular butter —
says, "More personality."

Memory: Each season labeled and saved.
There's that whale, my friend Elaine's long years
at Scripps in La Jolla, studying ocean resilience.
The small whale took up residence there,
and I, even as stranger to science, could visit.

My one scientific attempt was the display
of various molds growing in Jello, collected
for Campfire Girls when I was twelve.
The day of our meeting was warm; the Jello
had melted before I could show how bottom-of-shoe
grime morphed into cellular pattern. I'd had such hope,
such faith in the natural world to be stable, not fail me.

Nature's indifference stuck in my fast-changing,
clumsy, too-tall-for-my-age body. These days,
I understand that Nature won't give me more skill
than I have, or more time. But Smokey keeps singing.

* * * * *

I'm at home; I'm safe for the moment,
only hearing bad news, not in its streets
running from gunfire and bombs and a van
plowing into the people of Nice on treasured Bastille Day
In Turkey: a *coup* gone awry. Year of the Fire Monkey,
year of the worst. No one can think beyond fear.
Where is the cadence for that tuneless song?

What do we offer our anger and grief?
I'll give you this summer memory: I did a stint
teaching high school during what should have been my vacation.
One boy, when we went to the library, would not check out a book
because he'd never read one all the way through. Why ruin his record?
Why make a fool of himself with his ignorant buddies?

A friend staying with me during that summer
said later, "You left every morning in fresh little dresses.
I was jealous of you. You had a profession. I hung around smoking dope."
Then, I was angry at her for her own stupid life.

I tried to be kind in that library, but I quit teaching high school
beause I'd had more than enough resistance to wisdom.

* * * * *

More memory, more summer:

The year I was eight, I nearly cut off my thumb.

The year I was fifteen, when my mother was dying,
I spent the summer playing Canasta with Mary and Bobbi,

new friends in the city we'd moved to.

Right after college, I came to LA – June, 1960 –
spent summer looking for work, renting a place of my own.

My thumb still shows the scar where the long flap of skin was restitched.

Mary and Bobbi and I: The card game was boring;
the summer was boring – or, no, it was desperate but quiet.
My mother at our house. The cancer had spread. I had no way
of knowing how to be helpful to dying. I never had
knowledge I needed when I could use it. At eight,
I whittled, the knife pointing toward me. At fifteen,
I had no conversation, no comfort, to give to my mother;
Bobbi and Mary and I never talked, either.

My first full time job was a puzzle of law and insurance.

There came the summer when everything changed:
1971 – I'd made the mistakes that had to be made.
I paid for those, as everyone does. I'd become
an adult, earnest and burdened. A husband had left me.
I decided to write and continue to write and write a lot more and never stop writing.

Today, as I come out of sleep, one hand finds its other,
gnarled fingers sweet proof of a self. Arthritis
re-designs knuckles. I like being old; I always
discover my body's re-shaping. No clothing quite fits.
Those fresh little dresses replaced by loose-fitting
ones, patterned by women in India. Not quite exotic,
not quite routine. If you want facts, look at an old
person's body. Night before last,

I dreamed a man with curly, abundant black
hair. As I watched, he snatched the wig from
his head, stood bald, staring right past me, into
the waiting unknown.

July slips gently aside, with its poets,
its good Chinese restaurant. We talk
of the *daimon,* inspiriting force; we

sing "Happy Birthday." How many times
have I sung this old song? When I return
to the past, it's never the past; it's time piling
onto itself: The texture fills in the melody,
remembers the words.

2.

August 1st: Lammas, first harvest, sacred to pagans —
first loaves baked from new corn. The Celtic sun
poured itself into such corn, gave all it had.

August brought me my husband —
Harry and I came together a week past a rainy deluge,
unplanned by the forecasts just as we hadn't thought
we would have lunch, then a life, a whole

life in the pleasures of language and sex, the roses
he loves. Even today, right this minute, he's brought
home three blooms, set them in water, made them at home.

Loyalty, heat, admiration — sometimes total collapse
from the surprise brought by love — Our private harvest of sun
in our bodies grown suddenly stronger, suddenly bold.

* * * * *

Tonight, August 11th, will be the annual Perseid
Meteor Shower, the most powerful in years. Go to the desert
where no city lights fuzz your clear vision; stay up
until past 1 AM; face away from the moon. Watch

the shower of fabulous lights. The whole thing, though, is dust,
and the lights vaporize in an instant. This miraculous sky-show —
simply dead dust. Sometimes, we're fooled:

When I was twelve, I was allowed to go into the circus's
"freak show." I'd begged to do this for years. One memory
stays; it ruined the childhood of circus for good:

"Turtle Woman" was really a woman, a dwarf is
my guess, crammed into a big tortoise shell — head,
arms, legs sticking out of the holes as she crawled on the platform
above a sparse crowd. Her face was the face that Fate gives
someone who's cursed by her time and her poverty —
a black woman, ashamed. We were led to believe
Nature had made this strange creature; I was frightened,
not really sure what she was. She wasn't a turtle.

She wasn't a freak. I wasn't supposed to be staring at her.
Science, which gives me the facts of the Perseid Meteor Shower,
takes all the fun of pretending it's wizards or gods or great magic.
We can harmlessly lie to ourselves if we like. But then

there's the charlatanism of freaks, and of greed. Making
a profit from shame.

* * * * *

"Return," threaded through summer:

My mother's Charleston, her pleasure at teaching me how
I could do it. The small whale at Scripps, smart in his bid for affection.
Continuing grief: my cut thumb; my dead mother; my first
job — a bad fit but it led me away from itself, which is how
destinies tame us and guide our poor choices
toward remodeled ends. The Campfire

Girls: They believed in my wits, in my progress,
that a bunch of us kids had the power to do what is hard,

make use of our brains – learn about firewood,
analyze books. On the same page of the Campfire
Girls Handbook as my failed experiment with molds
are these I could try:

"Make a steam turbine." "Fingerprint a snowstorm."
"Show that sound travels." "Put on a chemical magic show."

I come back to the Campfire Girl motto: WoHeLo:
Work, Health, Love. So overly simple. So unhip.
And still mine.

3.

Jean, my favorite first cousin, dies at age ninety:
pneumonia, old body giving in to itself, its insistence
on ending. As all of us do.

After the phone call, I sit, recalling the farm
where Jean and I rode on a horse who was named Aristotle.
We sang all the songs that Jean knew, being older than me.
I learned how to get on the horse, how to hold on.
How to listen to someone who repeated the words
of those songs till I had them by heart. Heart's patience,
heart's cousin.

Jean was the last one who'd known me since
I was born. So, here, now, is memory's blank space sitting
beside me, the onward forgetting; the voiceless, long quiet.
I write myself forward from that.

I write to put everything into the language I heard from the time
I was born, until English became my whole mouth.
My first word was "car." I said what I saw zipping by on the street.
I matched what I said with a true, common thing:
"car." I found joy in the sound of the car, in the word.

4.

September's long heat – I rely on the old Japanese *wabi sabi:*
beauty is deftly cracked pots, uneven pathways.

Old, fragile bones: the newspaper drawing of "Lucy," our
African mother, her half-us, half-monkey curious face –
she probably fell from a tree, broke too many bones to survive.
That's the latest assumption from studying all that is left of something
we need to call "Lucy" and "Mother." We carry her knees and her stare,
her earnest not-quite-understanding.

* * * *

A few days ago, it was August but now – it's a whole different spelling.

Tuesday's ripe moon: crescent above Dodger Stadium.
The weather predicted: not terribly hot, although September's
our hottest, most miserable, sweat-smelliest month. But each
year, there's one blesséd day when everyone sniffs
autumn's first turning toward us, the odor of cookies
and much better movies. Today comes that hint, autumn's
first flip of her hand, not quite a wave but nothing else, either.

I sit with my lunch; suddenly, outside the window, clouds take the sun.
The light creates dusk hours before dusk will be here with us.

Tomorrow, the moon enters a "void of course," day,
meaning nothing works for us; nothing against us. Standstill.
But new parsley, new thyme, rosemary, mint all look glad
to be where they are, spreading themselves in big pots,

Occasional days do feel less burdened than others:
Herbs planted right before there's a void.

5.

Autumnal equinox: this Thursday morning, not too early
for me to be up and about in the house. I clean out old
medicine bottles; I can't use what's expired.

"Season of mists and mellow fruitfulness," reads
the first line of John Keats' "To Autumn," the poem
I recite every year at this time, although his England's
no kin to two palm trees set against clouds,
straightened beyond possibility; yet, here they both are
for us sojourners to find in our own autumn poems.

PROFUSION

1.

Today's "O" in October: the wheel of the year
is picking up speed, exactly like two skinny boys
outside the window: short sleeved white T-shirts, over-long jeans;
their ages the time when nothing quite fits. They're caught
on the wheel, just as I am, as all of us are in our weather's terse blue.

This lunar month for old Celts marked the dream-veil's quick thinning;
Gort, which is ivy, opens the door — then twines at its closure.
Be careful: We've entered Hekate's landscape, its never full light,

never straight fact. Wait until midnight, then use her black pen to write her a note.
Sign it, "with darkest respect."

2.

Last October was anger and loss. Today, all the pumpkins
have come to the stores. Orange: the "O" of profusion,
year's harvest as roundness, fat circles to show us
we always return, knowing how little space can exist
between earth and its crows who rush toward our dead,
dead who can read what we send in the beaks.

My password some days is "solemn," and some days
is one long, blank sigh. Some days, I pour myself out;

most nights, I recall that the ancients hid their bare faces
from horror, from Hekate's death-giving mood:

Persephone is dragged, once again, to the Underworld: to Hades,

her husband, god of all souls, where she reigns
as soul-goddess, eating red pomegranates: The red
is an unlit version of color, invitation to stare,
wonder what souls really look like if this isn't it.
I believe that it is — the roundness — the wheel —
an inside packed full of seeds which any soul knows
as the start of what's coming to birth. Don't worry:
Mysteries have their conclusions, which aren't ever answers.

Gravity, weakest of forces, does hold us in place. Even the crows,
sleek and bombastic, settle onto phone wires above me,
say they need angels to help with their messenger work. I can't
summon those forces, but I can locate candles, which angels adore.

So, then, I do buy orange candles along with pale brown ones
like cinnamon sticks. I remember my friend who wished for
a magical life. She died young. After some years, I dreamed her:
Andrea waited across a broad river for great celebration:
She'd become Queen of Halloween.
We simply worshipped her power to enchant.

Why am I sure that dreaming redeems what we need?
Because I would rather believe than to give in
to fang-hiss, to a shudder brought with the winds,
our ghost Santa Anas; give in to our fear that the unknown
is blasphemous, horrid — a bony-sharp fingernail scratching
against our safe door. The unknown is only tomorrow,
which does understand who you are, what you deserve,
what you can't live without. You will keep living until your last day;
then, you'll join what you've wished for.

No, of course I can't prove it.

3.

October 12th: The moon visits our window.
She's heading toward full – in another three nights,
we'll have round and spectacular moonlight which
wakes me then sends me to sleep once again:
a kind moon, non-glaring, intelligent brightness
offering comfort in spite of the world's broken song.
Yes, She can bring destruction – controller of tides –
but not at this single moment when arrival means
waking in bed, seeing this moon through the window.

We can depend on the moon, and on the seasons.
In this shaky October – political rancor; anniversaries recalling
horrible break-ups; a friend unable to see; everyone's knees giving out;
my collection of scarves collapsing in color-strewn ruin – The whole point is this:

With earth's tectonic plates shifting beneath us, we still
can rely on lunar arrangement, on something alert in the dark.

* * * * *

One house in sunlight; the next house is covered with shadow.

I go into the kitchen, think only of feeding myself.
Here are the pears. Then, there are eggs.

One high school friend, voted "The Hair" and "The Walk"
in our senior year, lived in a house with her parents,
a house where she had her own bathroom. That's wealth, I believed;
that's what you have if you're rich. I never had that, which now
has no meaning at all, since Carol is dead. Wealth grants some pleasures,
but nothing like brown, ripe Bosc pears, or like musing on crows –
crows who are yapping a lot in the street right behind me.
They see into their crowness,

what we yearn for with mantras, sincere meditation, religious
retreats. We try, bless our hearts. Crows stare into themselves

without sin, take what they've got, fly it up to the souls
who are waiting for them. This year, I've lost three women to death:
Maude Ann. My cousin Jean. Carolyn See, whose
writing life mattered. Maude Ann gave me

a couple of secrets. Jean was a sister. Carolyn wrote
about Harry's day when small press magazines were given
their due, editors talking and talking. Carolyn writing it down,
getting her article into our *LA Times,* which never attends
to the poets right here, doing more work for the city
than anyone knows. The poets: our crows. Poets handle

the angels with deft caw and sparkle.

4.

Mid-day, I sit on the bed clearing my mind –
but I fail at this clean, simple practice. The truth:
I love thinking. I sit on the bed, waiting for Harry and groceries.
When I hear the door open, I give over to putting away
cartons of milk, fresh salad greens, frozen "Skinny Cow"
bars that I love. I love chocolate. Thinking and chocolate.

5.

Marvin Smalheiser has died. At his funeral,
there was a rabbi. There were his students –
in the past, I was among them – who, at his gravesite,
performed his beloved t'ai chi. Marvin, crusty old Marvin,
taught me t'ai chi with the patience he had when he knew
someone took that art seriously. I did, having to learn it
then learn it again and again, since I was older than anyone,
since I was never a dancer or athlete whose body
remembers whatever is shown once or twice.

Marvin said that Confucius said,

"Some people learn after one or two tries. Others
take many, but everyone ends up knowing the
very same thing." Marvin stood with me, holding
my elbow when I nearly tipped over trying
to lift my right leg, turn it a little, set it in place,
lift my left leg, turn it – such easy moves, but
failure for me. Yet, I did make small progress
and again more small progress until I could do
Yang Style Long Form with the others.
When I am asked about my religion, I say
I'm a Christian Jungian Taoist. The Tao is because
Marvin taught me t'ai chi: turning a leg one way
then the other. Since Marvin has died,

I've found a prayer that is Buddhist, because
Marvin said he was that more than anything else.
In the prayer, there's a wish for us to be "sorrowless."
When I think of the deer who once dashed through
the grass where we practiced t'ai chi – its marvelous
grace, its animal strength, I think I can move more
toward sorrowlessness, accepting what I am given:
slow progress or smooth, leaping joy.

6.

Dia de los Muertos and here's my long list of those
who have mattered to me, who are dead, whose names
I recite, adding some every November 2nd. I read out loud,
take my time – then, I come back to November's profusion,

October's bright "O," meaning orange pumpkins,
harvest and everything Keats ever wrote.

7.

Early morning: light against the pale wood of the house
across the street – religious light, the daily rapture.
When I was first writing poems, a well-known
(and still pompous) poet told me never to use the words
"light" or "dark" in a poem. His point was cliché, Romantic swoon.
I tried in earnest to find something else. But there are no other words
for miracle light on an old house, miracle
darkness waiting all day to be called what it is,
to get darker and darker until we have

winter solstice. But, we anticipate light:
spring fashions itself from stories of life
beyond life – miracle light, spilling from hope.

A terrible time here on earth with wars
that don't wear themselves out, don't
wave the accustomed white flag to surrender
toward mercy. Here in our country:
presidential disaster, fraud at Wells Fargo,
thousands of homeless here in LA.
Elliott, homeless, tells me a little
about his condition, then says, "I'm a man. I can take it."

Really? Should any man have to sleep on the corner
of Sunset and Vine? Collect bottles and cans
from the trash to make a couple of bucks?

* * * * *

Donald Trump will be president of our country,
of our angry, fed-up-with-how-things-have-been voters.
Winners or losers, no one is smiling. No one is safe
from rancor or protest, gun-murder or opioid death.
Elliott, though, still says, "The Lord has been good to me."

Donald, for God's sake, do some noble thing

to enourage our generous goodness, our peaceful
intentions. I'm waiting. So many are waiting.

8.

November: Profusion of thank yous,
profusion of gripes. Are you grateful
for, or do you complain about

weeds, parking spots for the disabled,
hot chocolate, our recent immigrants,
rising avocado prices? Thankful for
or angry about legalized dope, garden
gnomes, high heeled shoes – really
high heeled – exercise bikes,

Walt Whitman, persimmons, old hard wood floors,
bandages, ankles, dogs and their yawning, sermons,
dyed hair, silent movies, fast food, tape measures,
snow globes, mud flaps, minimum wage, or communion?

You can be in the "holiday spirit,"
or you can slam your own door, read
every book James Joyce ever wrote
while these final days of 2016 slide by
on the big city streets or out in the alley
where you put the week's trash. November's idea
that we have to be Pilgrims who've lived through
hard times and now give our thanks: We are not
those brave, those insufferable rebels.

My husband watches a movie in French
about the Resistance fighting the Nazi invasion of France
which isn't as far in the past as the Pilgrims and needs to be heeded.
We'll never be safe,

so find what you want to do with November,

do it before you are stopped by fear or
distractions, your mother's request that

you roast the turkey this year — *you* host
the cousins and sweethearts and crass hangers-on.

* * * * *

November's profusion: I tear fresh kale
into a bowl while thinking I'd rather be reading
a book of De Lillo's I've got on my book pile,
but, really, I'm happy tearing up kale into small
and than smaller green bits for Zen salad
relying on tiny then tinier leaves,
grated carrots and finely chopped
mushrooms, etc... etc... etc... Domestic
attention or excellent language? My kitchen
contemplative self or my swift mental
pleasures? I stay with the kale.

* * * * *

French lavender fields stretched beyond
my young life when I rode past them,
past color I've never forgotten. Lavender
ruling a world whose language made
mine feel like limping and falling.
I loved the strange trip, one I'll never repeat;
I loved the whole fish, boned with such expertise
by French waiters. I love lavender still,
so I pull out a bottle of lavender oil from a drawer,
inhale, remember what's gone: travel,
the sandals I wore, finding a life-sized
gold statue — Jeanne d'Arc — half-hidden
in old Notre Dame: The woman who dared
to follow her voices and never recant.
Lavender spreading its pleasure for miles
upon miles upon miles. Sacrifice made

to the fire of all but her heart. What
makes us human: surrender to beauty,

staunch anguish of faith. Divine Mother Nature
and God of our Fathers: Whatever we worship
makes us its own. We can have both or we can have
multiple heavens, or we can have nothing to do with religion.

November's bright lesson: Everything's true if you smell
its ripe fragrance thousands of miles from the source.

9.

All day, the wind has been blowing and blowing,
discussing the strength needed to keep us alert
here in December, when profusion is weather,
is re-reading the novel I've wanted to get to for weeks.
December brings us more lights than we need —
it takes pleasure in blowing electrical fuses,
blinking along with old songs, "Chestnuts roasting. . ."
my favorite, but I also like hearing our cheap
snow globe play half of "White Christmas"
each year. I just wind it up. I shake its fake snow
over the small, silver reindeer inside. I can hear
half of "White Christmas" whenever I want to,

whenever I sit with December, listen to wind,
fear for our plants toppling over. Last year,
I sensed angels and crows as December's winged spirits.
I still do. The crows, though, are scarce, and angels only
appear as a piped in rendition of "Hark, the Herald Angels
Sing" at my dentist's. While I have a crown re-cemented,
my dentist tells me she's roasting a goose this Christmas day.
"Dickensian," she says. Yes, pull out *A Christmas Carol,*
tale of greed given up for remorse. But why not

angels singing from now until new year's?

I don't need morality; I need celebration.

An occasional crow – one, two – maybe joined by
another – but sparse. There's no point in requesting
their presence. They love what they love,
know nothing besides brilliant crowness.

Hurray for such diligent instinct-respect. A better
example to me than fusty old Scrooge, surely worn
out from years of misanthropy then humble reform.
Who wants to repeat that over and over?

If you want suffering, think about Jesus.
It's his time of year, if you're Christian,
which I sort of, pretty much am. I do think of Christ,
puzzled about all his mystery, his human-divine presence
among us. You can read him as myth; I take him as fact,
fall for the story *en toto*. I like Jesus: the manger, the wise men –
their gold, frankincense, myrrh. The star above shepherds,
the babe with his mother – Madonna and Child:
repeated in art over centuries now, much better
than Scrooge's yearly appearance.

* * * * *

4 AM, I'm out of bed to turn on heat in the living room.
Two patches of light brave the cold to sit with our ceramic
cat Buddha – I want nothing more:
We've done what we can for this year.
Tony, the friend who knew that he hated me
loves me again. He'll probably hate me again –

we shift as the world rocks on its axis.
"Did you expect this?" one of his t'ai chi students asked
Marvin when we brought food for his birthday.
"I don't expect anything," Marvin replied. That
seemed to me an intelligent answer. Now, Miles Davis plays
"Night in Tunisia," which I wasn't expecting, myself,

until I snatched the CD from the stack on my desk.

Tony's loving return to my life:
He's proably dying, but maybe — who knows?
Diseases decide for themselves, leave us
with weekly injections and making amends.
I'm sorry he suffers. I don't trust the love.
The hate wasn't trustworthy, either.

We shift as the world rocks on its axis.
We've left Tunisia. We've left the concert
Miles gave — Harry won tickets — Miles alive,
wearing gold. Playing the way he is now.
The album photo is him: a young man, mouth slightly open,
ready to lift his horn to his lips. The bass player takes over,
moves us right through the next track.
"Night in Tunisia" reigns as the hymn of the season.

10.

One mother walks with a red Santa hat
in her hand, her child next to her heading
for school down the block. Then, a mother
and six-year-old hurry along, both wearing
their Santa Claus hats; the child's is low
on his forehead — of course, it's too big.

We've had a full "super moon," which occurs
when the moon is closest to earth: a fine gift.

If there's no snow in LA; we get rain and a moon.

If there are no reindeer, LA does have coyotes —
and I have a big bowl of ripe tangerines, ready to eat.

* * * * *

As we drive home from shopping, Harry
turns on the radio. Dizzy Gillespie is playing –
what do you think? – "Night in Tunisia," our hymn.

Yesterday and today, I solved two problems of outage:
a fuse, then a plug fallen away from its outlet.
I am invincibly useful, at least for two days.
Doesn't this go with the season?

Here's winter solstice: North of the Arctic Circle,
solstice brings no light at all. Here where I live,
it was gray in the morning; then, we had rain;
now, we have more. There's a heater next to my feet –
no Celtic bonfire, but it serves the same purpose:
We can remember the warmth that returns in the spring.

The day after the solstice, there's lunch on a patio,
opaque glass between us and inside of the restaurant.
Reflected: palms lift behind me, magical genies
ready with fortunes. On the way home, city-scape
sways through the car window: my long, rippling
history here in LA. Some days like this are best seen
as wavering mirrors – all things predicted, nothing yet sure of itself.

* * * * *

This week, a radical Islamic terrorist, Anis Amri from Tunisia,
drove a van into Berlin's Christmas Market, killing thirteen,
injuring many. Anis Amri himself has been killed.

"I thought Tunisia was romantic," Harry says,
watching the news. Had Amri any idea that his country
has been given music outlasting hatred and war?
That his actions, horrific, do nothing to stop
Miles Davis recordings, Dizzy Gillespie, our sacred listening?

11.

This window lets in, now, cold air.
Harry wants freshness;
I give myself over to ironing clothes.
We breathe, and we smooth what we can.

MOTHER OF US ALL

1.

"I always like the sunshine on the houses across the street,"
Harry says, early New Year's morning. I do, too.
Craftsman-style, wood-construction, well-porched houses
where their owners have settled in like those sturdy bushes
fronting the porches' length.

The beginning year helps us reconsider:
Kathleen tells me *Calm* had a damaged cover, so she bought
Joy. She gave me *Love,* each day a quote from a better
soul than mine. I could never think of 365 messages of love
set down to inspire, encourage, make me more loving —

although I've been loved: My mother listened to me without judgment.
My first best friend taught me how to laugh at Ogden Nash's
silly verse. In fifth grade, my teacher came to my ballet recital,
surely a ridiculous parade of little girls in wobbly slippers. Then,
she wrote a thank-you note. Okay — these are my inclusions
in my year-long book: You can call them "love" or "joy"
or "calm" or anything you please. Harry calls it
sunshine on steady houses.

* * * * *

As I grew up, my mother let me sneak
dabs of her perfume; I bought her White
Lilac for birthdays. She bought herself
White Shoulders, knowing more about
the body's pleasures than I could quite

imagine. Our mothers showed us

how to shave our legs, buy bras,
wash monthly blood out of our panties
with cold water. We ate Campbell's Soup,

homemade pies. Aunt Jeanette's black
walnuts from her tree for cakes and cookies.
I believed movie musicals were grown up life
I could expect. America was perfect as it was,

except for everything we didn't see in movies
or in our public, white, all-Christian school.
Separation of the church and state? Not at Hartley
Elementary, where the Christmas play rated
as a Big Event. One year, I wore my mother's
sequined rich-green formal, hemmed; I was
a noblewoman bearing gifts to Baby Jesus,
whose manger was in Hartley's auditorium.

I was cautioned to walk slowly, nobly.
Whatever "nobly" was, it was uncomfortable.
I'd requested a classic sweatshirt, gray, for Chistmas.
I rode my fast bike anywhere I pleased

until I felt my body weaken every menstrual month;
until I fell onto my bed, stared out the window,
wondered what had happened. There wasn't
pain. Just puzzling melancholy, lack of

energy to get my bike out of the garage,
pedal to the local park and back. My beautiful
maroon Schwinn bicycle, my closest relative –
until my hormones took its place.
I had little bras covering the body's secrets.
Being a woman meant being a secret, hidden

in modest underwear and loose wool sweaters.

I bought dressy shoes with one-inch heels,
as high as I could walk in. I took a class
in ballroom dancing. I wasn't having fun
but taking step after step into deeper silence.
The line between me and everybody else:
permanent blue ink from a fountain pen I cherished,
carried with me every day, back and forth to junior high.
A pen became my bicycle.

* * * * *

If this New Year starts with girlhood,
it progresses in its second week to
rain, release from five-year drought,
sloshy tires against the pavement out
on Mariposa Avenue. Ardent rhythms
matching my CD which plays Hildegard
von Bingen's chants, sung reverently
by four devoted women – medieval specialists –
harmonizing in St. Ursula's hard story of virgin martyrdom.
She refused to marry any pagan, even a prince.
Maybe Ursula missed out on romance, or maybe
she went straight to heaven. Powerful faith deserves respect,

as rain deserves our reverance, deserves
religious gratitude. Anybody who complains
should just shut up. We need this more than
we need dying trees, the dead-grass lawns. With rain,
the yards across the street – fallow, spiceless brown –
have burgeoned into Irish green, a green that sings along with worship.

Here comes another car, splashing *amen.*

2.

I'm alerted to a TV show defining God. The conclusion:
"consciousness survives" after these present lives.

Last night, sleepless, I turned in bed,
wondering about this possibility.
Then, I heard my mother's voice:
She said, "I'm with you." These words
have never come to me before.
Completely audible, repeated
several times. She died in 1954.

Has she been waiting, alert,
until she knew my friend had said,
"Consciousness survives"?
I slept a little, not the whole night through
but enough to get me into morning.

3.

Harry brings home roses
with the yogurt and the toilet paper
and the walnuts. Red, red, red, these
flowers set in water, accompanied
by greenery, now on our table
in the place we keep for loveliness.

Kwan Yin, goddess of compassion, meditates
with the Cambodian wooden Buddha in our living room,
a corner where some sacred objects gather, including
an orange pumpkin from the fall which keeps its freshness
next to Mr. Buddha (as I address him every morning).

Kwan Yin, great meditator with her patient strength
may save us if we let her, if we keep ourselves attentive
to her myth: When Kwan Yin reached the gates of paradise,
she heard the cries of suffering people; so, she returned to earth.
She gave up eternal Something Beautiful for us. Her little statue
has its place right next to Mr. Buddha.

* * * * *

Harry said last night as we both fell asleep, "Adios, day."
This new morning, he asks to warm my clothes
over our floor heater, which he does for his own shirt
and pants. We see nothing but politics grinding away on TV;
there's fear in friends' voices as they give reports
on Donald Trump, new president; on our country's horrible divisons.

I think of Anna Akmatova, banned from Russia's "approved"
list of poets, in poverty, in anguish for her son's imprisonment,
speaking her poems to friends who memorized her lines until
it was safe to write them down again. Lucky us, so far.
We are warming our clothes, taking our baths, watching TV.

Thousands and thousands

last weekend marched in the streets for women's rights,
for our immigrants, for the natural world, for little knit hats
keeping their ears from the chill. I marched through the Sixties
with that era's causes and slogans: anti-war, pro-civil rights.
I haven't forgotten that nothing is solved. There's a new documentary,
"I Am Not Your Negro": James Baldwin's life:
Here he is again in front of me, reminding me how ignorant I am,
always because I'm white. I'm angry, too, James Baldwin,
with anybody thinking that I'm wrong to be exactly what I am,
what I can't change: to be a woman; to have an old, infertile body –
I don't own houses or a business, a portfolio with thick investments.
We live here in East Hollywood, which a restaurant critic once described
as, "a decaying neighborhood." She should have seen that we're Latino,
Filipino, Peruvian, White, African-American, Armenian.
Frank, a handyman for our apartments, is Russian.
When I told another handyman that Frank's repairs
tend to be industrial-strength but ugly, Ruby said,
"Soviet Union." Frank had sense enough to leave
that stifling regime. Here in East Hollywood,
I'm the lucky old lady at 1256 N. Mariposa Ave.
with the enormous metal shower head. Thank you, Frank.

* * * * *

I already have two lemons; I think I've asked that
two more be delivered. What's delivered: a bagful,
stuffed with yellow lemons. How can I make
use of these? So many ripe lemons, so many, many lemons.

Awake, I remember someone wise telling me
about too many lemons from her tree:
"I like to put them in a bowl and look at them."

Natural beauty, not always to be used but to be admired.
Plump lemons piled in a bowl, lemons just to look at.

4.

I have two more dreams of gifts to go with the lemons,
the many, many lemons:

I sort through soaps I have, deciding
what I need to buy. Then, just behind me,
I see new bars, delicious smelling soaps,
the ones I love. Where have these come from?

Then, the final dream: *I check a pile of panties*
in my drawer, relishing the clean pairs, thinking
that I have enough, although no woman
ever has enough of favorite panties, and
yes, suddenly, right next to these I find
a new stack of exactly the kind of panties
I have bought for years. Who has put them here?
Who knows what I want so intimately?

Awake, I write the dreams, and, as I write,
I realize: Only my mother would give me
sun-yellow fruit in winter, then fine soap along with panties
nobody else would think to place in this one drawer.
My mother obviously has been collecting evidence
of all the years she and I have been apart.

* * * * *

February, hinge which gestures winter into spring –
Not yet, not quite, but wind today sweeps the world brain clean.
Spring is never simply purple iris; it brings with it birth pangs,
pre-historic fetal growl, mammalian throb: those swollen breasts.

A man walks on our roof. He lops off overhanging
branches from the Chinese elm nobody can stop.
Elm roots tangle through our pipes, make our
toilet, sink and tub a mess of sewage. Above us,

branches cram themselves across the roof: scraping claws,
unwilling to give up until they're cut then piled
along the walkway, chopped into smaller pieces,
finally taken to the trash. The tree remembers,
though, how to make its branches and invasive roots.

I see we have just four more February days before
we're into March, month of the vernal eqinox, Nature's fate
combined with ours: Good or evil, whichever runs
along the psychic road, the future path. Children's
shouted laughter now outside our house could be
long wail, loud keening for their tiny past, five or six
or seven years they've lived, furnished themselves with memories,
learned to write their swift identities across the top of any paper
given them to hold their names, not let go.
Once we know our names, our private fate can find us.

* * * * *

A man once said to me, "Women smell like olives."
My menstrual blood carried the taste of iron. Why not be
earth's flesh – olives' salt and brine; iron's strength?

March, sacred to Mars, our necessary strength,
iron in the blood and this month's stone: Bloodstone,
symbolizing courage. I take my courage from my history:

Once, I cried as I watched junior high school friends
wave and wave, jump up and down until the train
was too far down the track for me to see them.

I cried as long as I could cry. Then, I forgot the friends,
the house I'd lived in all my life. Forgot our vacant lot's
catalpa tree; my secret lilac bush, the Civil War sword
in our basement belonging to my own great grandfather's
courage, not to mine. For the time I needed courage –
years – I lost the gift of crying.

In ancient Rome, this month began the year. It carries spring,
of course, everything's beginning.

The gods are cruel; the gods are kind.
What will it be today? This painting on my wall:
dark blood-red with something like the sun beyond it.
Blood mixed with light, today's first given.

5.

My thought a year ago: "Sometimes
the best I can do is shut up." I wrote this
as birds were swooping into spring, birds
throat-strong and whistling; every day, birds –
swooning, ecstatic. Music that verges on Lent:
sacrifice, dying, then miracle.

* * * * *

"Lumina": blue letters, painted across the side of a white van going by.
Blue sky. White, humming clouds. A van made of paint and sky, finishing
March harshness. Harry lights a white candle in front of my breakfast.

"With a candle, you're never alone," he tells me.
His love is always a mother as well as a lover to me.

(INTERLUDE: I'd left the family dinner to go outside. I loved my mother and father, the aunt, uncle and cousins gathered the dinner table, but suddenly I had to get away, shivering in the early spring Nebraska weather where patches of snow still lay on the ground, trying to melt but having a hard time of it. I headed for the alley that separated our house and yard from the Saunders', directly across from us.

I walked looking down, watching my step, not sure where I was headed. Then, in the middle of the alley, lifting from a muddy pile of snow, I spotted a cluster of Bachelor Buttons. Their blue was a vivid purple-blue, surprising and beautiful in the steadily darker evening. I knelt in the snow to look at the flowers, their ruffled petals like fragile wings. Even at age ten, I understood the moment: nature's ascendence out of winter's dormancy.

This was proof of God, no doubt about it.

I told no one. My family and I shared a mild version of Protestant Christianity, benign enough, but our Congregational Church never satisfied me. Divine revelation in a common flower would have made no sense in a religion of memorized prayer, solid good works. In college, I lost my religious faith completely. Our snowy alley had nothing to do with passing Latin Literature in Translation. On my small college campus, there was art, though: theater, painting, music, poetry. The arts seemed to me a world of Soul. How to join that world? I couldn't, I thought. I had no gifts large enough to offer Soul.

Ten years later, I fell from my Phi Beta Kappa rationality into emotional exhaustion. What gathered as despair became my gift to the Bachelor Buttons. To find my own religion, I had to live within my dream life, within my true love of writing, my pull toward myth, symbology, archetypes, alchemy, pre-historic origins. I didn't find The Answer but The Mystery, the Sustaining Mystery.

Bachelor Buttons are re-seeding annuals, returning every spring. Once, a long time after my vision in the alley, I wrote in a poem of mine, "I am returned to what I never left.")

DON'T MAKE IT HARDER THAN IT IS

1.

April is the month of Aphrodite: love.

Or, the word means "open."
Or, it's a Latin baby name.
This morning, early, I'll take "open,"
a fresh month for all of us:

Hold that baby, whatever name you give her
or him or the just-born kittens or any sentimental
sweet relief from scorn, self-mockery,
too much staring at this magazine, its pages
filled with tips for defeating online fraud.

Harry, as he tests the heat of coffee, slurps a little
at the cup's thick rim. "A lovely sound," I tell him,
and I mean it. To please me, he slurps again.
No fraud here, simply kitchen, alchemy of coffee grounds,
hot water, milk and sugar: a whole new brew.

I'm in the company of books written
by our friends: Jerry, Phoebe, Margaret,
Michael, Jack: the poets — along with Starr's
grand years of mythic research, unshakable enthusiasm.
To know these writers, to have their books as close

as reaching out, opening the pages. To read, that skill we offer
to our whole grammatic lives. Peculiar shapes like B or Q
suddenly aware of their own meaning: "bee hive" or "quilting bee."

Miss Smith, my first grade teacher, kept her patience while we
"sounded out" each configuration on the page. I relied on language
as the power behind adulthood. I understood that no one could grow up
without the newspaper or the Mother Goose rhymes in the book
I had at home, memorized so that the music and the story would unfold
a brand new self: Somebody literate. Somebody worthy.

At our local library, the Grown Up Room was beyond a flight of stairs.
The day when I turned twelve, could go upstairs and not be shooed away,
I entered Sacred Space: shelves and shelves of books I didn't understand,
books I couldn't live without. Later,

lonely in my adolesence – mother dead, father occupied with his new wife –
after school I read whatever books I found assigned, reading that transported me:
I was Eustacia Vye striding across old Thomas Hardy's Egdon Heath.
Years later, I would actually walk across a field toward Hardy's cottage –
a field buzzing with insects; the place as quaint as I envisioned writers' cottages to be.
Reading kept me in this world yet helped me leave it,

split open the vast fruit which is imagination.

The years when I took French in college, I yearned for some
pronunciation other than my own, but finally recognized Old English
as my bones – familiar, every syllable a shoulder or
a child to nurse – or Beowulf's refusal to give up.

When I, myself, gave up on French, I found the Beats:
hard-singing alphabet yet lyric praise: "Sunflower,
thou never wert no locomotive," Ginsberg wrote,
a line I memorized just as I memorized
the Mother Goose enchanting me through childhood:

"Hey, diddle, diddle, the cat and the fiddle."
Who can resist such leaps of faith? Sunflower
or whiskered animal, music played by fiddle, drone or lyre?

* * * * *

Druidic dream: I examine a twig for a long time —
an ancestor: "duir" which is "oak," becomes "door"
in Old English; twig becomes tree, is the door,
is the poem, is this dream reaching back, craning its neck
for thousands of years.

These ancestors buried ships loaded with their noble dead,
with gold and all the honor of their too-short lives. Why
such art, such thoughtfulness in warring people? Why such
poetry? Why write poems in our own dark age?
Even our comedians turn to hate for satire.

Yet, Alberto, Lebanese, who cuts my hair, still can sing:
He tells me he's performing at a local Coptic church
for Easter. Now, in Egypt, Coptic worshippers are bombed.
Alberto left his country when Christians found their businesses
destroyed, themselves unwelcome.

Alberto sometimes sings a bit for me in Arabic, allowing me
the melancholy, praising, passionate religious beauty of his life.

2.

Mid-April: Hard-breathing green joins with itself in stem and bud.

Tony is dead. He, whose nasty goodbye bruised
me enough to start writing this long (stem, bud,
flower unfinished) kind of poem.

Tony's true name is Gary, which I can write
not only because he's been dead four days,
but because I'm determined to speak about
him not as fiction but as a friend, whose final
appearance at our house for dinner came
with extraordinary effort — to move, be kind,
behave as if he'd go on living: We'd have lunch
soon at the restaurant I'd been thrilled with.

He'd be thrilled, too, always drawn to whatever is beautiful.
The night of our dinner, he declared, "I love fashion."
Barely walking, he still argued fiercely for art's highest standards.

Snobby. Ignoble. Narcissistic. Beloved.

"He's bleeding to death," said Robert, his faithful-beyond-
all-requirements love, keeping watch at Gary's bed
when nobody else wanted that work, the end work of death.

                    * * * * *

"Whatever we worship makes us its own,"
I wrote last November, just at Thanksgiving.

We worship the names no one will save
once this generation surrenders its place.
our ashes long ago scattered or buried or simply
shoved back in a cupboard behind
jars of spices and extracts. If it's true

that our consciousness stays in the mix, then
can we still learn? Can we still read?

"Don't make it harder than it is," I've titled
this time – since reading was easy for me,
why not stay with it? If we become what
we worship, then when my ashes blow
over the ocean, I'll be reading. I see

smoke dissipating, clarity washing itself
through my no-longer-body,
my new understanding: Word choice is God.

Right now, not dead, not yet freed of only one
language, I read translations: An Anglo-Saxon
poem calls someone egotistical full of "self-yeast,"
a perfect metaphor from fifteen hundred years ago.

Here at the end of April, wind flips Easter's quiet into breakage,
an upstairs window crashes to the walkway next to us.
Harry spots two men this morning outside pushing their car.
Suddenly, nothing works the way it should –

Gary's dead. After having him somewhere in the world since I was twenty-six,
it's difficult to think his ashes will be taken back to Paris –
Gary's wish, but permanently far away, old friend, too far away,
although you loved the spot where you will be.

3.

April slips inside itself, burdens relieved.

4.

Goddesses, gods are alive in old groves,
out of doors, not in confinement. I don't
have a grove, only a patio – full pots
getting fuller: Parsley and spearmint,
the basil already poofing its leaves to be
trimmed. Today, I am planting, arranging,

picking up wind-churned debris. As I pot
little seedlings, a white butterfly comes to watch.
This is Sarkis, Armenian neighbor until his granddaughter
came to our door, said, "Grandpa is dead." Armenians
don't tell me such private news; so, Grace standing
with me – a privilege. She added, "He'd want you
to know." That afternoon, a long time ago,

a white butterfly wouldn't leave me alone as I gardened:
Sarkis, saying goodbye. Today, then, I understand
who's making sure I do everything right: Druidic gods,
Sarkis, and probably Mary, the butterfly's wife,
who brought armloads of chard. She and Sarkis planted

and planted: even a fig tree that gave off a crop in no time at all.

All right, there's no sacred grove to honor this April's
slipping away, but honor can honor itself, sun drawing sweat
from my body, soaking my clothes. Nature, everything's yours:

living and dying and fertilized soil in my jumble of pots,
here in Los Angeles, here in the city of nervy ambition, of deep immigration.

* * * * *

May, its curious rabbits, the low-lying blessings —
nothing too overwrought, nothing far-fetched.
My birthday dinner: fresh salmon, potatoes, asparagus.
Harry prepares the whole meal. Come, May, lovely month:
your still-tender sun; grass underfoot a cushion-y green.

The Return of the Native, once romantic to me,
now seems like protein — builder of muscle.
Egdon Heath, a stern god, requires justice,
plus hiding a lot behind bushes to hear
conversations the plot has to have with itself.

I am filled with Hardy's descriptions — once
pages I skimmed. Diggory Venn is a hero, a man
I'd completely forgotten. No word of Hardy's has changed.
But I've added years of respect for what's valid,
what's faithful, endures: the Heath and its silence,
the characters' right to be bold as the Heath.

"You're not an indifferent reader," Harry says, as he
sees me holding the book on my chest, close to my nose.

* * * * *

For Sissy Boyd:

Jacarandas, moody sky – my friend and I over breakfast
consider our limping, our shuffling, our sexlessness.
But each of us smiles at the other's deep face,
at each year we have done this, each breakfast ordered. ·
It's always the same: the Figaro omelet and coffee –
cappucino or latte, thin slices of bread in a basket.

Our bodies forget us, but jacaranda trees bloom, rampaging in May.
We are only reflected color – the same moody lavender-gray as the sky's
drizzly clouds. *"There are so many details,"* my friend reminds me.
"Too many details." She thinks of appointments and banks,
how to call Uber or Lyft: When the driver has opened a door
for her to get out, she walks a not-too-smooth sidewalk into a place
that is strange to us both. She has a room; she has safety she needs.
We both disappear into age, the trees shedding purple and purple
till no details remain, only the flagrant, rooted arousal nature
insists on, year after year. Death and its opposite manage themselves.
Leave them alone. What we reflect is surrender, the grandeur of that.

5.

Southern California iconography: 5:30 AM,
full moon behind sky-tall palm tree. I'm awake
with nothing to do but watch until Moon has shifted,
leaves us to guess where She's gone. My window,

my church. Archbishop Palm and Priest Shorter Palm,
right next to each other. One morning later,

it's Sun rules the neighborhood, lights the red
roof, the brown roof until they are tributes –
not simply shelter. On this not-high-class street,
we still have our deities, our flowering bushes,
our sweeping and hosing to welcome Great Sun.

But admit it:

Moon; or thick-beaked god Thoth — ibis, creator of writing,
of restorative spells; or the bubbling alchemical cauldron
of possible gold — these powers shadow our naps; they sift
through the pages we've numbered, changing the order until

when we turn to the story we've written, characters
have grown extra eyes, can give birth to a crow or an elbow.

Great Sun slowly backs out of the late afternoon: We gave Him the morning,

now, we need to look into our favorite *grimoire,* definitions
instilled there by witches and seers, alongside the fat man I saw walking
today with his two toddler twins, a restless small fate holding each hand.

* * * * *

Look! It's the big man again; it's the twins:
Today, a black and white dog, leashed, follows
their rhythm of patience and hopping. "Once in a lifetime,"
I'd thought, the first time I saw them, but gods can be kind
just as gods can be cruel: What brings this fine trio to me,
plus their dog, for nothing except my spontaneous laugh when I see them?

How does the man hold each twin by a hand but
holds, also, a leash? Why doesn't anyone fall?

Now, the weather trades its fervent white clouds
for languish, for swerve. Sit yourself down.
Watch us collapse on TV, our nation
beswirled by its charlatan buzz.

"We'll just have to use a lot of underarm deodorant
tomorrow," Harry calls to me, between naps and asparagus.

A photo: chin on my hand, surrounded by books.
I wear a white blouse. A table loaded with food's

in the background. Poetry, Sunday, high temperatures bring out
sheer dresses, elegant beads. I think of Pompeii.

Sudden earthquake, erasure —

but photos could last in the rubble, no one identified,
but, still, archeological remnant — beads against blouse:
The end of ourselves, but I am eternally pensive, with books
stacked right next to my other, free hand.

* * * * *

I'm tired, too tired. As much as I want this
whole section of April, May, June to be about
not making things hard, things are hard.

I gave Robert the gargoyle Gary once brought me
from Poland. "Yes, it *is* Gary," he said,

then told me his plans to move soon,
go back to Redlands for family,
for flat, even ground. The treacherous
hills of Mt. Washington, our aging —
his already crushed hip — he was rescued
by Gary the day that he fell.

"Gary loved you so much," I remind him.

All is past tense about Gary.
I believe that he's safe.
I believe in the ancient, myth-enriched Greeks.

In their cool Underworld, I've experienced music —
the drone, elegaic — and goblets of wine older than living,
more scarlet than Upper World fruit. Gary would not be
unhappy with this. Persephone lounges beside ageless Hades,
assuming the role of a welcoming hostess.

We have this life, and we have others.
The gargoyle sits on its haunches and grins, has a thick dragon tail.

6.

It's June 9th – Clara's birthday, grandma who died
before I was born – although she knew I was coming,
the unexpected child of my long-married parents.
She and I must have crossed paths in the ether between birth
and the afterlife's wisdom because she's always familiar to me,
stout and impractical, painter of delicate china.

Once in a dream, Clara gave me a book of poems
that she'd written, although she never wrote poems,
woman whose photo shows her face windblown,
frowning and squinting. What did she look at to cause
her long beads to swerve upward, as did her hair in that wind?

When she gave me her poems, she passed along
what she hadn't done. Have I made her happy?
Prairie Clara, handing me poems yet to be written.

WHAT WE CALL EVERYTHING

1.

Alberto, as he cuts my hair,
says he believes it's "the beginning
of 'end time.'" He says, "Reach
out to God." He stops snipping,

spreads his hand broadly in front of me
where it moves in the mirror,
reaching toward God. "God is here,"
Alberto says, "always here."

He brushes loose hair from my face, trims back and forth,
uses a razor to shave little hairs on my neck. I stay very still.

I have no understanding of "end time,"
but my life as I've known it for thirty-nine years
will be finished, be rubble in just two more weeks.

I won't see Alberto again, or his wife Nina, who cut my hair, too,
for twenty-some years. "Reach out to God." Well, yes, I guess
that's the point. God's always here, Alberto believes,
unlike our monthly appointment, Alberto singing a little
in Arabic, a comfort for hair being cut from its source.

2.

The large — really tall, really fat — man with the twins
and the little black dog, spotted again: the boy twin loves

marching, knees high, and then yelling; the girl twin's bouncy,
short pigtails jump on each side of her head. Today, the dog
leads the whole family, quite stately, knowing his job;
assurance the day holds its place on this earth.

Then, 1:30 AM, after the Fourth of July fireworks' din
has subsided: Moon, golden egg, claiming Her place.
I wake up, glad the clamor has passed. Suddenly, earlier,
three awful booms with red smears filling our neighborhood
sky — I thought a house was on fire —
I thought the worst. But 1:30 AM: silence and Moon.

3.

I thought a house was on fire.

Then, there is actual fire, not celebration:

July 18th, 3 AM, one room of our house goes up in flames:
three walls loaded with books; my clothes, every
sweater and blouse and the black jeans I loved,
along with uncomfortable purple suede shoes, and, well,

what we call "everything" —

Computer. Printer. Desk lamp that constantly wanted to fall on the battered old rug.
Small sacred totems: My gentle brass angel; chakra stones set in a bag;
photo of crazed-looking guru whom I took as God's happiest self;
drawing of ancient protectress, playing her cello next to her wolf-dog;
Olivia's "Homage to the Creative," which had always hung on our wall —
its fierce golden mask wearing feathers. There's more:

Harry's early editions of Hemingway's novels. Kerouac's work. And poetry, poetry.

Gone with bad wiring is all that we've held in our hands,
read then re-read, syllables shredding themselves into smoke,
later to dust, even later, in two thousand years, breathed as clear air.

When I stare at the ashes after the firemen do what they can:
"It's gone," my first thought. I mean "gone"
as completed. Thirty-nine years in this house are fulfilled.
Destroyed and fulfilled.

* * * * *

Hekate began this whole year – October, 2016, days getting
darker and darker. This goddess who guides us through darkness
waited until I was living with nothing but darkness and ash.
She appeared at her crossroads. She smiled, not what
I had expected from her, but thankful she'd answered
my human anxiety: how to get home, whatever "home" will become.

* * * * *

Three weeks after the fire, after a neutral motel, after the news that our landlord
won't cover our losses, I have a cool cloth on my neck. Lunch never fails us:

There's yogurt; there's fruit; there are fans on the ceiling more often than not.
Our friends give us comfort, a bed in a peaceful, well-cared-for room.

In the place we called home,

we have to make choice after choice in the rooms that weren't burned;
why all this stuff when fire has taken so much? Let go of desire,
the fine Buddhists tell us; let go of stuff that we thought
made a difference, made us happy or brave or worthwhile.

Yet, one thing from the past – far in the past – does return
as miraculous history saved on a high, distant shelf in a closet
away from the fire. A photo of Clara, Grandmother Clara, young woman,
her face in my father's, in mine. About 1900. Companion to photo I've kept
of Clara as old. When somebody dies before you are born, someone
you really should know, you're "a guest on this earth," an astrologer told me.

My childhood retreat was our basement, where Clara's odd zither took up a corner.
I couldn't play it; the strings were too rusty. It had played, though, for her,

which meant she had touched it, had wanted this music.

4.

Fire trucks. Alarms. One ceiling crashed through to get to
the fire, contain the fire, let it destroy only this room,
this space of work, creative homage, creative resilience,
intimate search for the best word, the best view from the window,
the best shirt to iron, the best and the most and all that inspired
Harry and me toward belief in ourselves, in our still-fertile
minds, belief in the heart of our world, these books and this
writing – this life and the painting of Andrea's roses, the painting

her echo – this life and the postcard of women carrying great
jugs of water on top of their heads. This life with Harry's commitment
to what he and David and Don began as a record, a blog, now
a success measured by how many poems, how many poets have
filled in the years, lifted our cultural standards – Wordsworth
and Keats, Duncan and Levertov, Kyger and Homer.

* * * * *

This afternoon, Gelson's, the parking lot seething with cars;
Harry runs in for a boxful of strawberries. I wait.
I like waiting. I like its work, Hekatean, the crossroads, where no one
can pass without observation. Gray-haired woman sits at a table;
sunlight increases the green of her T-shirt. Another woman, long dress,
lugs two paper bags full of groceries. She walks quickly, and,
when we finally drive up Griffith Park on our way to the freeway,
she's still walking fast, getting those bags home to some place

I've never been.

Then, revelation: What no one can guess.

ANOTHER SKY

1.

A squeaky bird I can't quite see. Leafy shubbery I can't name.
Our wooden Buddha's shoulders — sun-warm when I reach for home.
So far, T-shirts and pajamas are in drawers. I've found Andrea's
small batik, forgotten until our former shelves were emptied.

Here's a mossy heap at the bottom of this palm tree — "palm":
one name I recognize as Southern California, the landscape
just beyond the mystery shrubs. 7 AM, I arrange my chair
to watch the day begin its Sunday self. I fold my long gray shawl
around my shoulders, think awhile about my friends, now souls:
Andrea's great wish: to live in the imagination, make iconic fabric cats,
batik mandalas, paintings affluent with roses in illuminated vases.

Ah, Romanticism, such a blessing when your body falters.

In the middle of Los Angeles, I looked straight up the street,
found Griffith Observatory, our local saint, worshipping the sky for us.
Here, though, in a place named for the woods, this other sky brings out
its fleecy grays, nomadic whites. Suddenly, a wedge of geese flies overhead,
greeting all those clouds with honking — full arias above the greenhouse
and the garden plots, the mound beneath the palm.

I belong now to an island where the language is familiar but holds a new vocabulary.
"We've got buckets full of hundred-year-olds around here."

* * * * *

This new life exists for us because Harry's been an actor —

movies and TV – so many years. Because of him, we're welcomed
in the Villa, part of a larger Woodland Hills Motion Picture and Television Fund,
a residence which has everything we'll ever need. I've had two other miracles, years ago;

this third, exactly like the others, relied on perfect timing:
the match-up of events, of personalities, locales and mercy.

* * * * *

Several mornings from the geese, enough wind to call this truly autumn,
alive now in my wish to put on a dress I haven't worn before:
leaf-woven print in auburn, black, reddish-tan, smatterings of yellow.
Added: a pin with feathers, beads, a tiny Buddha swinging in the center.

"Putting on The Glamour," as in putting on the Goddess:
chosen clothing, potent decoration: requesting courage
for the day from More Than What I Am Alone.

Outside, the wind brings out a monarch butterfly,
sudden flight, wildly orange and black –
but then it is itself, a leaf I've only seen as wings. The leaf
and not the butterfly lands against the shrubbery next to me.

Still, the ordinary is transformative, as I, in my autumnal dress,
have caught a glimpse of spirit-butterflies. – the wind,
such shaking and arousal, brisk eloquence –
the chimes next door: melodic chorus only when such wind arouses them.

Andrea herself appears: She's the resident black cat with four white paws.
Andrea revered black cats, believed they were the best luck possible.

2.

Final sacrifice of what we've left behind: Clara's big handpainted platter,
grandmother I never knew yet loved because she painted every dish she could.
The platter – always the bearer of Harry's and my Thanksgiving turkey:

There was the year someone recited a too-long prayer, deftly interrupted
when the turkey threatened to get cold. There was the dinner headed for
an all-out argument when one guest said she hated Michelle Obama.
Then, we had Thanksgiving when six guests became fifteen,
which didn't matter because Florence told me,
"These are the best green beans I've ever eaten."

I think now of the platter in the trash. My hands over my face, Harry, who's driving,
notices and says, "We wouldn't be human if we couldn't be heartbroken."

3.

In this unexpected sky, long cloud ribbons, rose-pink sunrise
gliding in behind them – the filling pleasure we call "wonder."
We come toward Hallowe'en, Dia de los Muertos. My list of dead

recited every year, lost in the fire we had this summer. I'll remember –
or I'll be reminded of those names I do forget because the sky
gives up its knowledge as the days progress.

* * * * *

We've come into October's heat: We need patience,
lightweight clothes to help us breathe. This is the desert
where we live. This is the mythic visonary's landscape –
Hot, dry wind through history, biblical insistence.
I have no gift for wandering alone, but I understand
the value of the search. My hands are proof of that:

heavy-veined, arthritic – document and compass.
The past three months I have relied on perseverence,
written in my Taurus birth sign but needing practice,
as all religious effort makes its way by diligence.
The morning sky is cloudless, no advice revealed:
Blank and voiceless, leaving any messages to wind,
which brings to life again our neighbor's wind chimes.

So, music rather than thick silence guides me past myself
to breakfast – I listen as a woman at a nearby table
in the dining room tries to tell the waiter what she wants:
"Cereal," she manages, tells him to "put it in a bowl."
She stops. She can't begin again. Finally,
she gives up on her own words. "What is it
I need?" The waiter knows. "Yogurt," he suggests.
"Yes, yes, yogurt." The bravery of old age
is futility of pretense, clarity that comes
with saying, "What do I need?" How we can
answer for each other, make sure the yogurt comes,
along with corn flakes, milk and coffee.

Later, I pay attention to the few magnolia leaves fallen on our patio:
The velvet underside welcomes my touch; tough and crackly
outer leaf crumbles when I pick it up.

Strange collection that we humans are – so much goes on
without our saying yes or no: bodies filled with cells and water,
blood, extensive lungs, nerves and ancient DNA; or my mind suddenly
alive to seventh grade's insistent roller skating, the hot-pink baseball cap I wore
all the time I swerved around the rink. I trusted my strong feet; I still have

faith in any way I find my balance. Harry says to me,
"Sunflowers. Library. Looks like rain." So, here's the
vibrant stable world – no leafy crumbling, just things that grow,
along with reading, weather. Still, I can't ignore the Other World,

Celtic New Year: Souls are hallowed, never turned away.
I like revising, which is distillation, which is, I think, the swift, clean work of souls –
Nothing wasted, nothing overwrought. Add sweet candies, though, because
we need to know we're loved by more than one abandonment.
We mourn. Then, seasonal tilt:

My mother – in the handsome purple dress she wore on holidays –
can reach for me, remind me just what hands can do:

She made that dress. She set a sun-gold pin on its left shoulder.

Her hair was curled, hair a color I received from her: reddish-blond,
now faded, but restored in memory.

4.

November 1st: I thought the wall was tree. I hear
Cecilia talk but know she's leaving, that in another
half an hour this, too, will be a memory, like everything.

Like mourning. Yet, the little plant, a gift, which
seemed completely dead is watered and revived.
New month:

I thought the wall was tree; then enjoyed my own surprise
to see the wall itself, smooth stone not bark. The wall is wall,
but doesn't have a lot of purpose since it ends before it stifles
any freedom; you can walk right past it to November 2nd,
Dia de los Muertos. I find the dead and living close together,
mingling, greeting one another, no fixed boundary, although they know
this doesn't last. We get one day a year. One visionary slant of air.
Welcome, darlings, and farewell again. Yet,

Andrea's batik mandala has been hung where I can look across
the room, remind myself what lasts is artfulness, devoted color –
After her struggle to stay here with the living; after the death she didn't want;
after Andrea had made it into What-Comes-Next, I dreamed her cured,
her cancer gone, her body perfect: The bedroom where I found her
deserved the title "boudoir." She took Romanticism with her, but
left me this mandala, fine purple circle enhanced with blue and
white and lavender. Stir the colors any way you please, they last.

* * * * *

Full moon at perigee, closest it ever gets to earth.
Full Beaver Moon in Taurus, industrious.To Wishram Indians,
"Snowy Mountains in the Morning" moon. Harry points out
the moon to me, a moon I have no private name to give,

but I can sit – two nights – to watch whatever happens.
Moon stays her course; clouds dramatize. I look
until I memorize this moon:

full, round planetary jolt. Two nights after this,
moonrise has a different time: What had enchanted me is gone.
Somewhere in the middle of the night, not sleeping well,
I remember a time of having nowhere to belong: No one
I'd counted on would be my family or my friend again.
I was too young, but I knew expecting nothing
was the way I'd see it through. I got a job: I sold cheap jewelry,
blouses, hosiery when I was still in high school.

Nobody was especially kind, but I earned a little money,
realized that once I left the nothing-that-was-ever-home,
I'd earn some more, enough to be a person.
Moon always remembers to come back. I could rely on that.

* * * * *

Thanksgiving will arrive on time: There's no more to be said, except for me
the pointlessness – why one single day set aside for history and pumpkin pie?

However,

Charles Manson's dead, mid-November, 2017. Farewell,
that evil soul. Manson's women: They murdered at his bidding,
ended 1960s peace and love, flowers handed to the scowling cops
who lined the streets at protest marches. After Manson's spree,

no one, we understood, could trust the power of daisies. One friend
came back from prison in Morocco, bone-thin, hepititis-ravaged.
Her wealthy father got her out of jail, out of a sorry marriage to a guy
who dealt a lot of drugs. She'd been the one to preach get stoned,
kick-off-your-shoes, dance barefoot. Go somewhere exotic. She stumbled
back to us, reliant on her father's money, not on chanted affirmations.

Let me, though, say thanks to her because she left

a hefty, round, oak dining table. She left a typewriter.
She left a quite-new copy of the wise I Ching.
A few days ago, I opened the I Ching at random:

"Deliverance" was the hexagram I found. A loosening of difficulties,
plus advice: resume your ordinary life as soon as possible. Which
is my way to view Thanksgiving and the 1960s: resume what matters
every day. So, November

curves along its hallways, squeezes past us, doesn't say, "I'm sorry."
Months aren't history; they just hold a place, week after week,
for rattling events. More terrorists. More good deeds: a college
in Rwanda now for women to be leaders. More sunshine here,

the farthest edge of San Fernando Valley. I've returned
to Wallace Stevens, my abundant source – I have time to copy out a lengthy poem of his.
One large wish I've had for life is to belong to poetry, and so I do.
Happiness is danger, though, especially if your joy is language,
which is magic spells: poetry can conjure both the dragon and the harp.
(I thought the tree was wall. I found it wasn't; the wall has kept out nothing.)

5.

Now, November's been demolished; December's breath is smoke –
terrible wildfires carried by the Santa Ana winds, homes and hills
ablaze. Victims weep; somebody says, as someone always does:
"Everything burned, but we have our lives. That's what's important."

Sky, sky, wind, wind – the tallest tree, half-leafed, half-winter,
rides and shimmers. Yesterday's nausea has passed.
An annoying friend has been postponed. The Christmas tree is lighted;
I sing carols with others in the lobby of the Villa,
while homemade cookies make their way around the room.
The elderly blind woman next to me reaches a stuttery hand
along my chair, so I take it while we sing. She smiles,
not knowing whose warm hand is in her own. I've forgotten
more song lyrics than I'd thought. Forgotten the pleasure of familiarity

when it comes to holidays – each person sets a shiny ornament
somewhere on the tree. Holding hands with anybody next to you.

Clouds today: spread out as thinnest silk. Sunlight jumping through
its kingdom, tossing random gifts to us – illumination worthy
of this vivid mid-December, 2017. I'm not ashamed of loving beauty.
I'm ashamed of missing more than I can see.

* * * * *

Winter solstice comes and goes. Here's reassurance,
a specific time to praise the earth's lopsided circling. I read
that *mundus imaginalis* – world imagination – will save our species.
Yes, yes, it will. But 8:27 AM on December 21st, this year's
solstice moment, saves us, too. Some holy days are simple practicality:
The planet's still in business.

This week and last, there's illness here among the Villa's residents.
So, we're being quiet, solitary, fed from trays reliably
delivered by the waitstaff in protective masks.
We try not to infect each other with anything but cheer.
A new year's coming. There are medicines.
We are ourselves the medicine of staying still,
letting dark infection pass our apartment without stopping,
allowing our home planet to assure us that it's right on time:
Sky's oceanic blue shifts toward gray, then back again to brightness.
Sun lifts itself, even in this month of shortest light.

6.

A slow drive Christmas morning: A few miles west
and here is Southern California as I've learned its winter colors –
gray-green plus dormant tan on hills. Big hills, each in place,
companions but not leaning into one another. Steeply sloped
yet gracious: the formality of someone mannerly but distant.
This is my Southern California, semi-arid landscape bringing
chilly nights and mornings – then sun. Born to Midwestern prairie,

I've come to love both wintery subtlety and ocean: insistent water
challenging the silent hills. Extraversion/introversion: the whole imagination.

* * * * *

Hawk and hummingbird. Hummingbird and hawk.
Light sweeps across the tall magnolia tree next to our patio:
Everything's on the move. This other sky – so unfamiliar
in October – has become a neighbor. Whatever shaking urges
vast tectonic plates to realign our thinking, I keep looking at the sky,
which, nonjudgmental and astute, does welcome my regard.

Woodland Hills: From 8,000 years of Native American life to
the first Europeans – the Portola Expedition – naming this place
El Valle de Santa Catalina de Los Encinitos (Valley of St. Catherine
of Bononia of the Oaks) to the Mission San Fernando to Harry Chandler's
"biggest land transaction ever" in LA County (1910) to Victor Girard Kleinberger's
2,886 acre purchase: He planted 300 pepper trees, called the place Girard.
In 1945, it became Woodland Hills. We're in the foothills
of the Santa Monica Mountains, a comfort of boundaries,
of solid persistance through every change.

* * * * *

Finally, 2018 opens its blank pages. I dream:

Here is a roomful of art: As I enter, it's dark,
completely dark. But I cross the threshold anyway,
trust that the lights will come on.

MUNDUS IMAGINALIS (the whole imagination)

1.

We saw Buzz Aldrin hop in moon dust — 1969.
We know the moon as scientific fact. That's one reality.
Tonight, I sit outside in winter dark to let the almost full,
close-mouthed moon shine through me —
Her myth, my body: That's as true as knowing
Her broad surface harbors silica and iron.

David Hockney's etchings in a book of Wallace
Stevens' poem about the blue guitar — Picasso's
painting, eerily moon-like, the guitarist, blue —
blue as "blue moon." Once in a —

* * * * *

Moon boosts Herself through trees, above
the jacaranda into New Year's heady dark.
As She climbs, She rules the tides, the world.

Someone this morning wore a T-shirt with the slogan:
"The future is female." So is the past. So is this present time,
the effort of bringing a heavy year to birth. Think of it:
Moon, opening her womb to offer us what only She
can manage. A year, freshly given, which has the force
of cosmic management. Be careful how you spend these days;
they come from altitude and sacrifice. They come also

from our big Sun: Moon's presence seen by us because
of Otherness — We need such balance or we topple

into hatred. When I listen, this is what *mundus imaginalis*
has to say: "There are no enemies."

* * * * *

Creation has its origins in loneliness.
Creation has its origins in praise.
What will save our world?
"The vivid transparence that you bring is peace." (Wallace Stevens)

* * * * *

In January, we can think about the possibilities.
Orpheus, Divine Singer, changed Nature herself
with music: Trees uprooted themselves to follow him —
he held the power to persuade through wonder.

In our own hallway, a famous singer, losing memory,
never forgets her music. Suddenly, she'll sing whole
choruses for us, right on key. Orphic impulse changes her,
and changes us, her listeners. Now, in the *LA Times,*

remembrance of a Leonard Bernstein concert when the audience,
after a standing ovation, moved *en masse* down their aisles to be near the stage —
a whole crowd longing only to be closer to the music's source.

Shameless longing: "Vivid transparence that you bring is peace."

This afternoon, my fellow opera fan: "A little Mozart never hurt anybody."

* * * * *

Sunday, another Sunday, day to be tired, comfortable, mess around
with watercolors — visual pleasure. A friend yesterday said she keeps
herself aware of joy. We confront so much bad news: Sexual harassment,
North Korean nuclear threat, our stubborn U.S. Congress passing
only tax relief for millionaires. Syria: war's devastation. Myanmar condones genocide.
What will save the world? Not governments.

The effect sun has on birds: stronger light makes stronger song.
Stronger belief in *mundus imaginalis* gives us a stronger world.

Thoughts and longing; music and my amateurish painting of Great Hermes,
guide between worlds, friendliest of gods, maker of connections, bringer of
good luck. Icons and art, story and our urgency to heal through
sheer belief in the impossible, which gives companionship,
gives thinking
much more power than treaties.

2.

Yesterday, assurance that our guest knows everything.
He told us so. But then, he left. So,

now the only things I hear are Harry turning pages of the
LA Times and wind outside jangling our neighbor's chimes.
I sat there on the patio awhile ago; I thought of how we lived in trees.
How many greens are there? Blue-green sprucy tree behind the winter-barren pear
tree;
yellow-green – low-growing plantings next to me, some mix of succulents.

Darker, softer, spread-out-green above all this. I understand what living in the trees
was like:
straddling and balance; a simian's long arms to climb with, a nose for fruit.
We do remember every home, settling down among the leaves to rest.

* * * * *

Fog erases shadow, completes itself in gray,
color of lost harvest: Winter withholds its compliments,
reluctant to end the solitude of dormancy, of fog:
lack of contrast, lack of opposites.

Early morning, Figaro the Cat comes in to sit with Harry.
This cat lives down the hall, wanders where he pleases.
I do believe he's Andrea in spirit, her certainty: Black cats are lucky.

After years with our own cats –

wonderful animals, mercurial examples of doing what you please –
Figaro inspires Harry to sing, "Que Sera, Sera,"
making up lyrics to include the cat himself.

3.

Lizard; bird blast; yellow flowers on long stalks
bloom ever taller. Sunlight on my arms feels
not just warm but hot. We step toward spring,
although that's still a month away. But birds won't
be denied; the song is crazed, erotic. The lizard wants every pulse

of sunlight it can get, lies on the wooden planter box
for minutes – not the measly seconds usually offered
me to watch its lovely swerve. We're Southern Californians;
we think we deserve abundant light at least a few
days at a time in February. Maybe we do.

Maybe if I soak up the light for long enough, discover
what it says, I can redeem my selfishness, my joy
in living where I live while there is suffering,
suffering, always suffering. This week in Florida,
a teenage shooter killed seventeen other teenagers –
Plenty of grief and talk, candles held in vigil,
nobody understanding how to stop this carnage.
When gun proponents give our politicians
millions, nobody refuses. Nobody.

4.

Now, Ameen Alwan has died, friend for forty-seven years,
poet and gardener and gentle eccentric, he sent a boxful
of persimmons to us every year, picked from his tree;
spent too much money on postage for the heavy fruit;

but he wouldn't stop, made sure persimmons got to us.

Always, some were too soft to survive the trip, but the spilled pulp
was beautiful red-orange. The art of damage – another way imagination
muses on us. I'm sad that Ameen's "left us," as his daughter
phrased it on the phone. I'm sad we didn't see him over Christmas
when he was still okay. I'm sad that now his gifts will be

the dreams which might or might not come. I never know when
loved ones die how far away they go. The distance can be short,
the dreams substantial, or the journey can become an orbit
none of us who live can join. There's so much to learn concerning death;

the only way to learn it is to die.

Let us think of nothing but predicted rain, ever welcome in this desert place.

* * * * *

I write this to discover what it needs, this history/poem/private
forest canopy where I look across the psyche's landscape,
watch the details add to themselves until a shape emerges:

If I continually yearn for what comes next onto this page,
who can blame me? Hunger sent those pre-historic
people walking the whole world. Food, food – whether
hunted animals or books I read or – yes – a dream of Ameen's
guardians toward the Other World:

Four dream-women wore the gorgeous masks of those who
are allowed Divine approach to Mystery but protect their faces
from observing too much wonder. They know the path;
they'll show Ameen the place to enter his own Other Life.

I write this because I'd be disloyal if I didn't. Disloyal to Ameen, who saw
I was a writer. Then, he found the space to plant a garden –
mine to care for – because he understood it was another way for me
to serve a larger life than I had ever thought was mine.

To become of value, take on another burden.

5.

A dream-tree, gold: The tree planted where I look
each morning just beyond the garden plots and greenhouse. A perfect,
gold-leafed sphere to honor Orpheus, Divine Singer, he who brought the trees
to ecstasy. Also, Ameen: This tree his life completely lived,
a life of poetry and gardening. I can't ignore the placement of the tree
where I can see the dream each day. I'm not allowed forgetfulness.

We've made it through the iffy Ides of March. Now, we 'll have the vernal equinox:

Here is my childhood driveway lined with purple iris. Age five,
I had my tonsils taken out, stayed in the hospital overnight.
When I came awake, my father, next to my bed, held for me a big bouquet
of fresh-picked iris. I'd been so scared, so worried about being good,
not offending any nurse or doctor — tall people in their bone-white uniforms.
Now, I'd passed through that to Daddy saying we'd go home. When we did,

I opened the car door, dashed to my swing in our back yard.

Back and forth, back and forth — finally, my tonsil-less sore throat
felt nearly normal. I looked over to the driveway, saw the purple iris blooming there,
knew my father's big bouquet was right inside the house, set in a vase of water
by my mother. I'd been promised ice cream after lunch.

* * * * *

March 20th: At the moment of the vernal equinox this year, rain is promised.
Birds can't shut up. 9:15 AM, the earth relaxes into perfect balance.
I feel it. Brief and eerie and elating.

* * * * *

March 21st: I watch the rain come down outside. I think of fragrant
Eastern lilacs accompanying my family's iris, the early purple colors I adored.
Mundus Imaginalis: It is Creation as a fragrant color, some kind of plain old love
but shimmering, lodging in the hardest places in ourselves.

PASSAGE

1.

A Great White Egret appears beyond the garden plots
to make its careful way just past the entrance in the wall —
this bird, taller than you'd think: vigorously preened white feathers,
slender legs too (it seems) fragile for its weight but Egret

understands itself, takes time arranging all that lengthy,
curving neck, pointing the impressive beak (sharp orange)
a little eastward. Pause. Pause. Finally, it sets one broad foot
slightly ahead of the other. Another pause. Then, it brings its

other foot six inches forward, taking, at last, a step.
Each repeated step

makes the bird a bit more visible from our patio. I'm quiet,
not wanting to disturb Egret's deeply considered passage
of twenty feet or so. It manages its travel, slowly disappears
beyond the wall but leaves behind its fascinating drama,
one I remember as pure education for what's next:

I'll be eighty in a month. Eighty years old: I know how to pay attention
when an omen shows itself, sticks around like Egret until I get the point.
Extreme old age asks for Egret patience.

* * * * *

Another iris story:

In half an hour, I'm leaving for a medical procedure,

one I don't look forward to. Sitting again on the patio,
I watch a Villa gardener walk along the path leading
from the wall's square opening where Egret stood.

When he reaches me, he offers me an iris more purple
than I've ever seen, a color no human being could imitate.
"For you," he says. The man, Latino, middle-aged, in work clothes,
smiles as I take the flower on its long stem. I thank him, tell him
my mother planted iris every year. These Villa gardeners
talk with Harry about trees, tell him the names.
They're deliberate in their work, certain of every task
because they keep the world alive. They know the names of everything.
I believe they know much more, as people do who give their full
attention to our earth. In fables, nature is most

common and most visionary. Any plant or tree can speak,
can prophesy or warn or give advice. Of course,
the medical procedure goes better than expected.

2.

Harry says today, a day in early April, "I write better
when I'm reading poetry." Cecilia comes for lunch,
brings books of Carol's poems. I re-read Rilke's "Duino
Elegies," glad to have the angels in them, glad my own
work doesn't ask for Rilke's sacrifice:
earth-bound reason given up for other-worldly genius.

The names of trees are pleasure; so are the books we've
gathered since the fire last summer took from us three
walls of cherished poetry and fiction, essays
and biographies – we'll never get those bookshelves
back, but now we have enough: Rilke. Olson. Virgil,
Homer. Bloom's Wallace Stevens' literary criticism.
Three books by Carol Muske-Dukes, delivered by our
Cecilia, whose own poems lift us. The pile of ash left

in our study back on Mariposa is just that:
completely ash, impossible to glue together
or restore. It doesn't matter. Harry can still say,
"I write better when I read poetry,"
then read aloud Walt Whitman.

* * * *

"The Great Work Begins in spring,"
alchemy insists, season of first things:
seed, egg, first sign of the zodiac — Aries —
fiery arousal. Plant the seed. Crack the egg
to see what bird emerges. The future:
it will find us with its own new list
of orders, pleasures and embarrassments.

Everything is damaged by the nightly news:
more chemical attacks in Syria — what government
promotes the deaths of children?
Or any deaths of those it rules?
Politics can only make excuses or send bombs
or fool itself with definitions of "psychotic." Our current
history isn't social work; it's Biblical catastrophe.

Now, a 90,000-year-old human fossil-finger
has been found; Saudi Arabian desert
has preserved it, proof that our tribe walked
away from Africa earlier than supposed.
Why have we lasted all this time? War making?
Handy tools? Chants and prayer?

Hatred could have brought annihilation long
before this present spring. "Passage" can mean
"artery," blood flowing to and from the heart,
great metaphor for empathy. Medieval alchemy
didn't give the alchemists gold to spend; it rendered
the impurities from the *Anima Mundi,* our World Soul.
So, it ennobled the alchemist's own soul. Chemicals

and compounds were involved; metals changed from
solid righteousness to the liquid that would join with
other elements rather than attack them. This wasn't
about poisoning the neighbors and their kids.

3.

The new moon rescues dark
with more dark: For one night,
Sun and Earth are in sync
on Moon's opposite sides.
A single, invisible night
to herself, Moon's solitude
raises our tides. What is She
thinking to do that?

* * * * *

The pear tree blossoming white: gradually, gradually —
surely a cousin to Egret. Every morning, another
possible bloom, but no hurry to announce itself.

Many-branched pear tree whose shadows fill
the three-story wall beside it. Shadows alive
as the tree, shaped by light, shaped by roots.

When anyone asks why I'm a writer,
I tell a few facts but don't mention the gradual
self who unfolded — some sort of bird;

some sort of bloom; something the size of a morning's
quick glance in the mirror — how could I see the face
I have now? Yet, I was there on the shadowy branch,
there in the mirror. We carry ourselves, lived
and unlived, from the instant we're born. There's no choice —
we only have birthdays, fading from this year into the next.

The mirror fuzzes over, erases smooth skin I once had
so my old age has a chance to know what it's up to.
When I was thirteen, I believed I should smile like
Kay Turner, the popular girl. If only I'd smile,
I'd be liked. But the plain, solemn face I see now
soon gave up niceness: It didn't help me, really, to live –
There's always despair, an excellent teacher,
along with that difficult puzzle, forgiveness.

This season of passage presses my arm, guides me past Egret:
We have freshly formed Aries – The Ram charging the sky with its fate-driven horns.

Give us revival and thrust; the tall wooden Buddha that Gary
once brought from his travels. Dead friend never dead
but with me as Buddha. It's been over a year since Gary's
been freed from his doubt and his Vicodin habit. There's
no one to make him feel shamed; there's nothing to argue against.

* * * * *

Monday's Small Ode to Harry

How beautiful your slender bare feet
as you sing, gently, an old children's song.

* * * * *

Oh, the pear tree! Whiter and whiter: Its blossoms increase.

Nature's indifference – create and destroy –
belies Her insistence on beauty, which may sometimes
be love. "I love fashion," Gary admitted, the last time
we ever spoke. Fashion's impossible artifice – well, why not?

I loved Gary not for his taste but for his long conflict:

He searched for unsullied ritual: harpsichord lessons,
astrology, Catholicism, Buddhism, Mongolian travel –

but being American, gay, resisting convention, craving
the risks not of the hero but of the fool — holy fool —
he gave up when every tradition was flawed.

Gary could laugh at disaster, but could never stop
meeting his demons — their standards far too extreme
for simple existence. High Fashion:

attempt at disguise, extravagant unwearability
if you're only human. Gary could never be that.
He wanted perfection.

4.

White clouds today: white — also gray, plus the lizard
who lives in the planter off to my left, who comes to the sun
as his instinct demands. Now, somebody whistling.
Nothing replies. The whistle again, calling to birds who aren't there.
What is it not to be answered, no matter how often you try?

The truth of finely-honed instinct; the truth of rejection.
Marla, first muse, has now died. She lingered in bed
as long as she needed to lie there, asleep but not really
asleep, collecting her life before leaving. How like her
to keep us all waiting. To not give a reason for silence.

She called me "best friend." Well, I was. I sent her the cards
and the gifts she could never give me. I know: her depression;
her exhaustion before this last comatose state. I couldn't blame her,
but I felt like the whistling person with no voice singing back.

                              * * * * *

Full moon in Scorpio: Absolute yellow, no subtle intent.
This month, the moon is an honest, hard-working woman.
I reach toward our Buddha nearby: dark wooden cone of hard wisdom

on top of his head. Truth in his message, exactly the same as any good soothsayer,

any mad saint: "Know thyself, seeker"; check yourself out,
fellow pilgrim. This morning, Clara (my grandmother's name,
but Latina; still, a similar face) shows me her earrings for Cinco de Mayo
made out of thread: intricate web –

such golden circles created from nothing but what mends us daily:
honest, hard-working thread, twisted and knotted and turned until
it's all art. Mariachis come into the dining room – two trumpets,
one violin, guitarone, small guitar – men's fancy black suits
trimmed with silver – as they play, everyone whoops and applauds;
spontaneous dancing occurs; laughter – sudden enchantment.

When I moved to Los Angeles (the Latino angels are here),
I came to get warm, to slough off my bulky wool coat and my fear
that I wasn't enough for real living. "Real Living" means letting
music and angels come in, welcoming every embroidery,
plenty of improvised dancing. Cinco de Mayo recalls a small,
poorly armed Mexican Army overcoming a highly trained army of French,
double the size of the Mexican troops. That's worth two trumpets, a fat guitarone,

fast singing with thanks for impossible odds not going the way
reason predicted. It wasn't my reason that finally got me to buy
short skirts in the Sixties, finally wrote one single poem
that I could call "poem." It included a lizard. Today,

several days past the fifth of the month and its fun,
the senior planter-box lizard comes to the sidewalk
in front of my patio chair. He's on his way under the foliage,
has stopped to refill his reptilian body with sun.

5.

A soft spoken angel tells me to sit, just sit down,
pull back the curtain, asssuring myself that nothing has changed:
the bush, spiky and threatening next to red blooms

facing east toward whatever light that we've got for the morning.
7:30 AM, Woodland Hills, California: emails to answer,
a few things to buy, but no memories replaying
novelty tunes from the 50s while I slip on the loose,
short-sleeved T-shirt I've wanted to wear for this long day of heat.

Post Its and soap; toothpaste and notecards. Fill up the list;
today, we can afford even the treats.

* * * * *

The pear tree has burst into green. Every white blossom is gone.

Mid-May, a Sunday:

Next to our patio door, the magnolia tree comes into bud:
ivory nipples all over the branches: Diana of Ephesus,
goddess with breasts everywhere on her body, Great Mother
extending her arms as She has for thousands of years.

How can we think we're alone?
How can we misuse our natural world,
which is Hers? In this practical nation of thugs
who take what they please, who will remind them
they're stealing the sacred? Pear tree,

magnolia. Lizard and rabbit – and koi
in the pond not far away. These are
respected in my private world, but beyond
the high fence, snarled traffic prevails.

* * * * *

Kilauea erupts. For the next many weeks, our planet revises Herself:
Kilauea continues bursting and spewing. Lava crosses a highway,
runs to the ocean, makes "laze" – combines with itself and
the sea's pungent water, a potent chemical brew no one should touch.

We, too, are sea water,
blood and our genes, scar tissue and nerves –

Kilauea destroys herself as she has been. So do we human beings:
Each year, my body does what it's meant to be doing:
gets older, changes and shifts, releases the past
to make way for whatever is next.

6.

The magnolia's firm buds have loosened themselves:
white furls of bloom appear at the ends of more and more branches.
Each morning, I watch what's going on with this tree,
how much sheer power it takes to open a blossom.

May opens to June: Month of our solstice, month of high grace.

*June is the month I came to Los Angeles, passage into full time jobs, paying every bill myself,
finding a friend – Sue was her name – to drive us to the coast where we got a shuttle up a hill to
Positano's: coffee house with folk guitarists. Yes, there was a man who showed me how to
play "Go Tell Old Bill" on my cheap guitar. He would have liked to be with me, which would
have taken me away from one big mess, my first emotional disaster, but I would have had to
fail some other way, so I have no regrets. I learned the song. That's what matters, finally, and I
still sing it – not every verse; I can't remember half the words, but plenty does come back to
me. The song is sad; Bill dies. I like the minor key, the fatalistic melancholy. That mood does
suit me, Anglo Saxon that I am, staring out to sea, keening for everything that's drowned.*

7.

Whose are these neatly-kept, similar-to-each-other
houses on the residential street we're driving past?
What goes on inside of homes? Once, I dreamed
I strolled around at night, went into people's houses
just to look at what was there. No thievery, no need
to find a snack, no intent to move the furniture –
only curiosity: How do people make their lives?

In my dream, a man woke up, discovered me. I said,
hoping to explain myself, "I've come to tell you a story."
We sat in his living room, in darkness, where I told
whatever story dreaming brought to me to offer him,
this stranger in whose home I found myself.
The man leaned forward, didn't speak, but listened.

Why were the houses easy to go into? On the residential
street in outer daylight, I know that everyone's alarm is set.
But in the dream-home each of us inhabits, stories heal suspicion.

The dream itself was story. My writing it is story.
The man who heard me – never dreamed by me again –
took what we shared back to his bed, to his own dreaming.
Somewhere, he and I still dream.

8.

Birds lift from the jacaranda tree, then fly away.
Sky is always subject, never a verb. Verb is birds,
their flying and their disappearing. Verb is change.
That's what makes us sad, not sky.

9.

Figaro the cat, Andrea's enduring spirit, finds
a place to rest inside our gentle space, the one
large room we call our home – clean and book-
rich. When Christ says meek ones will inherit
earth, I think "meek" sits next to "nose in a book"
or "do your own work," so peace prevails.

I think "inherit" isn't owning anything but
sneaking up on greed to make it share the food.

After Figaro has rested, licked his belly-fur, seen
that Harry isn't here to pet him, he goes away again.
No apologies are offered; none expected. Each of us has tasks,
our day's agenda.

TAO TE CHING, MAYBE

1.

The Tao counsels against restlessness,
so I stare at our sky, its overworld seclusion:
flat gray, like primer. Later, lingering sunlight,
unenthusiastic. Nothing moves, not even
three-story shadows which always
have a thing or two to show me. July —

a monthful of events — the Fourth two days
away — historic battles, birthdays, calls to action —
but here: non-verbal baseball cap, a book on opera houses,
a little yellow slip of paper with two words from Charles Olson on it:
"Enyalion" and "glacis," which I'll look up sometime.

＊ ＊ ＊ ＊ ＊

This is the United States, as Independence Day
reminds us. We work to worship God; that's
how our Puritans defined themselves.

Today, one of the lizards made its way
into the shrubbery and up and up until it
poked its head above the greenery; it pulled its body
up as well, waited for a minute, then slid down again
into the shrub. That was its work this morning,
proving agility to itself — to me, the watcher. I'm coming to believe

these lizards like an audience. When they include me
in their climbing, sunning their cold-blooded

shoulders, that inspires my body, too, my work
as human arm and ankle, thumb

and ear lobes which I fill with silver earrings
to adorn whatever work I do today.

* * * * *

Tao for the day:

Over one hundred degrees outside.
Use common sense — make peace with
whatever seems possible. Don't be fussy.

2.

Summer: excessive heat; constant,
illuminating light — our shortest season
but the most attention-getting. If you want
to hide, avoid the sun's big spotlight —
stay alone, curtains closed.

Paris, the one time I will ever be there:
hiding was inevitable because I couldn't
speak the language. The anonymity of ignorance
is not the anonymity of grace. This was no vacation
but erasure, which, I suppose,

sustains my present wish to never travel.
I can be ignorant at home.
Here's a whole new week —
untranslated till I live through it.

I read some Gertrude Stein, not a foreign language,
if I'm patient. I wonder about diagramming sentences,
which Gertrude liked to do. Her great
joy was sentences — as she invented them.

In seventh grade, I was good at diagramming.
Adolescent puzzle to myself, I started
toward some understanding with noun
and verb, object (both direct and indirect).

The *Tao* requires no effort at pronunciation — just
diagram what spells itself, needing to be understood.

* * * * *

I hope Yasmine, Ameen's daughter,
will visit when she's in here in August,
when she'll bring some order to the cluttered
Pasadena house where Ameen gathered
much more *everything* than anybody
thought he needed. I find among my own saved letters
a note in Ameen's handwriting. Ameen's alive here
in his private slant of letters on pale yellow paper.

A youthful volunteer at MPTF tells me he and his friends
have never learned to write in cursive. They rely
on their computers. How can anyone exist
without the whorl and tilt of written lines?

The British Museum's room of manuscripts,
the same year I saw Paris: under glass,
handwritten books with many fascinating
crossings-out and notes. I took comfort
in all writers' stubborn wish to *get it right*.

Also, amazingly,

a manuscript of *Beowulf:* The Middle Ages' forthright language
ever-present with ferocious Grendel and his adversaries —
here's the mead hall: blood-drenched wooden floors; hell-hearted devastation.

Ultimately, many pages later, Beowulf does die exactly
when the dragon he is fighting dies. These two a pair:

violence and rescue; fatal hiss and hero's sacrifice.

Only fools allow themselves to worship fonts.

Beauty shapes itself from each mind's private harpist —
or from what I listened to this morning:

Insistent geese calling for each other in the distance.
These local geese spread their voices in the clouds,
so when those clouds change patterns, Goose Talk changes, too,
becomes not honking but Old English.

3.

Last night's full moon rose in an unexpected piece of sky,
lifting slowly, not in shyness but wanting us to yearn for it —
gold-orange, fruity — summer ripeness after its eclipse that morning:
not witnessed here, but, elsewhere, moon erased and then released.

4.

July demolishes itself with fire: The Carr fire
has burned 100,000 acres, demolished
10,000 structures. Then, Mars: closest to our earth in years:

Check the eastern sky tonight, watch
the red emergence of the planet we imagine
might have life. Not "Martians" with antennae
in their heads but tiny microbes, microscopic somethings.

Wildfires, heat, firemen dying in the blaze.
Silent Mars, ever ready for our hopes.

August brings more heat.
More fires.

5.

August weather years ago:

My first library card got me
to the "children's room,"
a cool retreat with books I could take home —
miraculous to read the many books I chose then
take them back, get other books. Summer meant
shorts and sleeveless tops, words I didn't have
to look up in the dictionary unless I wanted to.
Sometimes, I wanted to. Sometimes I still want to —
Charles Olson's words:

There's no "enyalion," but Enyalius is Ares,
god of war, so there's a bit of info. And "glacis,"
(long *a*): a bank sloping from a fort exposes
anybody who climbs up. Reading on,

there's more Enyalion, who is Enyalius,
war god, High King. "His color is beauty,"
Olson insists. A warrior himself, plunging straight
through the field of the page; every story takes its chosen place,
makes no excuses. The Word: enchantment, wizard's spell.
I hate war, but under story's spell I don't judge Enyalion,
who discards his clothes while standing on a hilltop, making sure
his army and whoever happens past sees his full beauty —
masculine nerve to stand completely naked, be seen,
make a statement: "I am a god."

* * * * *

Harry brings home dahlias: magenta, blush-pink.
"They don't last long in heat," he tells me, but "Kiss the joy
as it flies," Blake wrote, so he puts the flowers in some water,
lets them have whatever life is in them to fill us the way words do —

in childhood libraries, or in the magazine I'm reading about divination:

"Clairvoyant Reality" in which the object merges with the mind.
Flowers, gorgeous and impermanent, belonging to their
knowledge of themselves, passing that along to us.

Within each stem, each word: a brain, a hive.

* * * * *

The *Tao* reminds me to yield, which seems easy
at eighty years old. The *Tao* is a cure for heady ambition:
There is none in aging since nobody's looking my way anymore,
no one needs me to win, wants me to lead that big revolution we thought
we'd pull off in the 1960s. "Oh, gosh," Harry whispers, as he lies down
to nap. This part of life gives us the privilege of rest.

6.

The one note I have from Ameen, written
by hand, tells Harry and me how glad he is
we're okay after our last year's apartment fire
took our old way of life.

He says he most fears an earthquake. Now,
Ameen's dead, so his fears are at rest.

I don't spend much time on fear; fear prevents
nothing. I don't spend much effort being nostalgic,
although I wish I had all Ameen's letters sent since we met:
1970, winter, five or six poets meeting to talk about poems.
I had opinions but really knew nothing. Ameen disliked me.

Then, seeing, I guess, how quickly I learned to shut up,
he could accept me. He gardened. He wrote. He fell
in love with a woman, also a poet, who played flute.
They married, gave Yasmine her life, then divorced.
How simple that sounds. Adding the details

would mean a long novel – a trilogy, maybe. What it
comes to is this: I counted Ameen as one of those
people I needed. He showed me how to be quietly odd,
stubbornly non-technological.

There's no prize for just living your life, but there should be.

                          * * * * *

Today, the pear tree is full of summertime green – bold green,
shiny with sun. Blistering sun has browned the magnolia's white blooms.
Our planter box lizards have found a new home; I haven't seen
them for two weeks, at least. Hypnotic green, overworked sun,
lizards' unexplained absence: If that's not a poem, I don't know what is.

Wildfire summer: the fire-ravaged landscape with nothing ahead
but to wait for new growth. Something has ended, something not yet begun.
While I wait – while we all take a breath –

think of that city in Kansas buried for hundreds of years,
People and rituals and potshards and legends. Conquistadors' written reports.
Think about *your* city burned out or buried, your lifetime erased.
Your habits, your thousands of meals. Your children's much thought-about names.
Your language, along with your hard drive. Your last illness.
Your loved ones' clean-smelling socks. The neighbor with freshly-baked brownies.
Your one birth certificate swearing you in to your time, your own astrological sign.
What are you? A Libra? A Pisces? Not anymore.

7.

Tao for the end of August

A workman appears, climbs
the three-stories-tall palm tree
behind the magnolia. Thick rope
holds his waist. Heavy boots
keep him from sliding. Electric tree trimmer

hangs on his belt, but he's able to clear out
debris from the tree's top fronds with his hands.
Tough chunks of bark spatter the greenery
below. Two huge, dried-out fronds follow this.

The high, leafy mound at the base of the tree
holds a fairy hill. Fairies are smart; they know
the workman is saving their home from
the rats which breed in the palms. Fairies and
workman together: acceptance of that which is Other.

8.

Good luck all around: In another two days,
a lizard appears from the big planter box.
Tiny, a child, it scurries along the broad
wooden rim of the box, letting me see
it and its family still thrive. Then,

On Friday, I'm being guided across MPTF's
verdant grounds by a man who points out plants
I might miss: rangy anise; superb, fragrant
rosemary. Even tomatoes right over there,
behind a wire fence. We see gardeners
washing away marks on the sidewalks
left by this week's tree trimming: heavy, dropped
bark on the path that we're taking south to the lab,
where I get an x-ray, some blood tests. We are all
Nature's work – our fast lizard hearts,
our blood, our dense and susceptible bones;
the bark of the palms leaving its history,

just as our wild DNA carries reptilian evidence
plus our hominid yearnings for large, better brains.

9.

September arrives: Like every new month,
glad to emerge. But then what? September
is tired of the old "back to school" theme
or Labor Day Bar-B-Que plans or comments about
"the autumn of life." September wants to exhibit
its power, gathered since Romans called it by name:
"seven," meaning the seventh month of the year,
(although now it's the ninth). September likes being seven,
the long reputation that number has for good luck:
Trinity/Quaternity added together – like workman
and fairies, opposition transformed into One Holy Thing.

Sure, we can announce what is Holy. If the gray, overcast morning
turns silver, isn't that signal enough? I'm not enlightened,
but I am an Observer. So are we all. Holy and Holy and Holy.

* * * * *

The moon, waxing, shifts in Her sky,
creamy as milk from the cows of my childhood –
milk, warm in the throat, generous glasses my aunt poured for me.

Moon and Her milk: mysterious
gift – another two days She'll be
bright in those trees that have bloomed
but aren't blooming now. The Moon
makes their worn branches shine.

We come to this year's autumnal equinox:
The Moon transits Pisces, which helps
us turn toward our harvests, the what-
have-we-done-with-our-time as the year
bends and sways, preparing to balance
itself, insisting that we come along.

This time of year holds all the secrets,

saves them so we can reach through the vines,
go farther and deeper, grasp every fruit we've been picking,
become the whole ripeness ourselves.

One secret is this:
You will feel your desires as completion tomorrow when
everything holds you together for one single moment.
We've already settled into earth's orbit. Give it a chance
to pursuade you. Equinox day:

Sun on dry weeds, making the stalks
equal in beauty to still-fertile green
that grows next to their dying.

Now, simply carry this equinox
balance through to the end of the year.

About the Author

Holly Prado (1938–2019), grew up in Nebraska and Michigan; she made her home in Los Angeles since 1960. *Weather* is her thirteenth book.

Her poetry and prose appeared in numerous publications for more than forty years, including *The Paris Review, The American Poetry Review, Temblor, Bachy, Askew, Exquisite Corpse, Cimarron Review, Poetry International* and many others. For nine years, she reviewed both poetry and fiction for the *Los Angeles Times* Book Review. For three of those years, she wrote a column reviewing new books of poems, focusing on books from vital, American literary small presses.

Honors include First Prize in the 1999 Fin de Millennium LA Poetry Award, sponsored by the Los Angeles Poetry Festival. Additionally, she was a winner in the "Sense of Site" project for 2002: poems by eight Los Angeles poets were printed in an edition of 10,000 postcards and distributed throughout the city. In November, 2006, she was presented with a Certificate of Recognition from the City of Los Angeles for her acheivements in writing and teaching, as well as her influential participation in the Los Angeles literary community since 1970.

Her poetry is available on the solo CD "Word Rituals," produced by Harvey R. Kubernik, realeased by New Alliance Records.

She taught writing in many educational situations. For twenty years, she taught poetry in the Master of Professional Writing Program at USC. Her private writing workshops went on from the mid-1970s to 2017.

Prado was living in the Motion Picture and Television Fund, Woodland Hills, Ca., with her husband, Harry E. Northup, a film actor and poet, at the time of her death. They were both founding members of Cahuenga Press, which has been publishing books of poetry since 1989.

ALSO BY CAHUENGA PRESS

Specific Mysteries
by Holly Prado, 1991 (OP)

You and the Night and the Music
by James Cushing, 1991 (OP)

Ordinary Snake Dance
by Phoebe MacAdams, 1994
(no ISBN) $10

The Ragged Vertical
by Harry E. Northup, 1996
(ISBN 978-0-9649240-0-0) $15

Sacrifice
by Cecilia Woloch, 1997
(ISBN 978-0-9649240-4-8) $12

Esperanza: Poems for Orpheus
by Holly Prado, 1998
(ISBN 978-0-9649240-5-5) $12

The Length of an Afternoon
by James Cushing, 1999
(ISBN 978-0-9649240-6-2) $12

Homelands
by Jonathan Cott, 2000
(ISBN 978-0-9649240-7-9) $12

Dreaming the Garden
by Ann Stanford, 2001
(ISBN 978-0-9649240-8-6) $15

Reunions
by Harry E. Northup, 2001
(ISBN 978-0-9649240-9-3) $15

Tsigan
by Cecilia Woloch, 2002
(ISBN 978-0-9715519-0-9) $13

Livelihood
by Phoebe MacAdams, 2003
(ISBN 978-0-9715519-1-6) $12

These Mirrors Prove It
by Holly Prado, 2004
(ISBN 978-0-9715519-3-0) $20

Undercurrent Blues
by James Cushing, 2005
(ISBN 978-0-9715519-4-7) $15

Red Snow Fence
by Harry E. Northup, 2006
(ISBN 978-0-9715519-5-4) $15

Strange Grace
by Phoebe MacAdams, 2007
(ISBN 978-0-9715519-6-1) $15

From One to the Next
by Holly Prado, 2008
(ISBN 978-0-9715519-7-8) $15

Pinocchio's Revolution
by James Cushing, 2009
(ISBN 978-0-9715519-8-5) $15

Where Bodies Again Recline
by Harry E. Northup, 2011
(ISBN 978-0-9715519-9-2) $15

Touching Stone
by Phoebe MacAdams, 2012
(ISBN 978-0-9851843-0-8) $15

Oh, Salt/ Oh, Desiring Hand
by Holly Prado, 2014
(ISBN: 978-0-9851843-1-5) $15

The Magicians' Union
by James Cushing, 2014
(ISBN 978-0-9851843-2-2) $15

East Hollywood:
Memorial to Reason
by Harry E. Northup, 2015
(ISBN: 978-0-9851843-6-0) $20

The Large Economy of the Beautiful:
New and Selected Poems
by Phoebe MacAdams, 2016
(ISBN 978-0-9851843-8-4) $20

Solace
by James Cushing, 2019
(ISBN: 978-0-9851843-3-9) $20

For each book ordered,
add $5.50 (shipping & handling)
and send to:
Cahuenga Press
1223 Grace Dr.
Pasadena, CA 91105

Most titles also available from:
Small Press Distribution
1341 Seventh Ave.
Berkeley, CA 94710